THE MARINADE COOKBOOK

Henrietta Green

Harper & Row Publishers Inc

to Phil, who patiently advised, ate and commented . . .

Acknowledgements

I would like to thank the various authors and publishers for allowing me to quote from their recipes and due acknowledgement will be found in the text; the various restaurants who have opened their kitchens to me; numerous friends who kindly contributed their favourite marinades; Karen Thesen, my editor, whose patience was a tower of strength; and Eileen Self, who typed the manuscript and struggled with my appalling spelling.

This book was originally published by Pierrot Publishing Ltd in 1978. It is here reprinted by arrangement.

© Text: Henrietta Green
© Illustrations: Tony Moore

First edition HARPER & ROW, PUBLISHERS, INC 1979

ISBN 0 06 011553 5
LCCN 77 11534

Printed and bound in Great Britain by Hazell Watson & Viney Ltd, Aylesbury, Bucks, U.K.

Cover illustration by Tessa Traeger
Colour photographs by Tessa Traeger
Line illustrations by Tony Moore

CONTENTS

Introduction to Marinating

When I told my friends that I was writing a cookery book about marinades, they all thought that it was a good idea but that I would never collect enough recipes for a whole book. I was able to reassure them on that count and in point of fact could almost have filled these pages twice over!

Marinating is based on the simple principle of soaking food in a chosen liquid so that it will absorb the flavours, give off flavours and become more tender. The liquid or marinade can be made from many ingredients and for the purposes of this book pickling, sousing, soaking in brine or a dry salt or spice rub are included as marinades.

There is a long tradition of marinating; the Chinese have been marinating for centuries and some of their famous dishes rely on the ingredients being carefully marinated before cooking. They marinate before steaming, so that the food has been aromatized before coming in contact with the steam, thus giving the dish a more complete flavour. The Indians, who love hot, spicy food, often soak their ingredients in spiced yoghurt or a richly flavoured oil, to ensure that the ingredients blend and all the tastes are released and mingle together. I also learnt about marinating from French and German cookery. The French are known for their sophisticated cuisine and rely heavily on marinating in wine, oil and herbs. The Germans prefer rougher flavours and use vinegar or beer as the base of most of their marinades. The Scandinavians pickle meat and fish, presumably to tide them over the long winter months when the lakes are frozen and the sea unfriendly; whereas the Arabs tenderize their meat for immediate cooking.

A well-balanced marinade will enhance the flavour of any dish and it is becoming particularly important as the quality of our meat and fish declines and the price increases. Due partly to the practice of freezing meat almost as soon as it is slaughtered, and to the feeding habits of intensively-reared animals, meat is often rather tough and tasteless – a marinade will help to change that. Also in these cost-conscious days when we are all struggling to feed large numbers in the face of constant inflation, a cheap cut of meat or a piece of fish can be transformed by a marinade; chuck or frying steak can be made as tender as a piece of fillet, and that is no extravagant claim.

Any dish which is to be marinated does require a small amount of organization – the ingredients do have to be bought and prepared well in advance – but it is really not too much trouble and well worth the extra effort and forethought. The times given for marinating in the recipes are quite flexible and can be adjusted to fit in with your schedule. For example, if I am going to be out all day I will prepare the marinade before I go and leave the ingredients to soak, knowing that on my return I can quickly and easily cook a delicious meal. If you can't face the thought of preparing a marinade just after breakfast (and if you have overslept you certainly won't have the time) prepare the ingredients for the marinade and the main ingredients separately the previous night and mix them together before you leave the house.

There are a few simple do's and don't's to marinating. Always choose fresh ingredients; vegetables and fruit should be firm and unblemished, fish should have bright eyes and be firm around the gills and meat feel and smell fresh. If you are using frozen fish or meat, do make sure it is thoroughly de-frosted and wiped dry before the marinade is added. Clean and wipe all your ingredients dry before marinating because if they are wet they will lose their texture. Always marinate in a non-corrosive dish (glass, stainless steel, porcelain or glazed earthenware) and always leave the dish uncovered to allow the air to circulate. Never add a cooked marinade to the ingredients while it is still hot, always allow it to cool first. Make sure that the ingredients are well coated in the marinade and if it is convenient baste them occasionally with a bulb-baster, pastry brush or metal spoon, or turn them in the dish. Always, unless the receipe specifically states otherwise, marinate in a cool place, such as a larder or a fridge. Allow a little longer for the marinating if the ingredients are kept in the fridge, as the temperature will slow down the process. Obviously the longer you marinate a cut of meat, fish or chicken the stronger the flavour – but there is the danger (particularly when using oil) of over-marinating so that the texture is completely ruined and the flesh will reduce to a soggy mess while cooking. Never freeze uncooked ingredients in a marinade – always cook the dish first and then freeze it.

Marinating can be used to preserve, tenderize or flavour ingredients. It should be thought of as enhancing rather than disguising a taste and that is why the balance of ingredients is so important. Herbs, spices, oils, wines and spirits are used to infuse and season – the result is a well-balanced dish with a perfect complement of flavours.

As I said at the beginning of the introduction, there are far more marinade recipes than I could have possibly included in this book, so if I have ommitted your favourite, please do not feel too insulted. I did try to include as many original ideas or adaptations from foreign recipes as I could, which I hope will give you all an exciting view of marinating.

Equipment

The only special equipment needed for marinating is a container made from a non-corrosive material such as glass, stainless steel, porcelain or glazed earthenware. It can be dangerous to use any other material, plastic is corrosive – that is to say can be dissolved or eaten away; aluminium, cast iron and copper are liable to rust and can leave an unpleasant metallic taste, and unglazed pottery is an absorbent surface. Glass, stainless steel, porcelain or glazed earthenware are rust-proof, non-corrosive, non-absorbent and hygenic materials and, as such, they are the only ones which should be used for a marinade.

The size of the dish will obviously depend on what is available and what ingredients are to be marinated. As a general guide, I prefer to use a flat, shallow dish for pieces of meat or fish and a deeper bowl for whole joints and fruit and vegetables. The animal ingredients must be "allowed to breathe", so ideally should not be piled on top of each other; if this is unavoidable, turn them occasionally so that not only will they receive a thorough basting, but the fresh air will be able to reach them. Never cover the dish containing a marinade as it must always be left open to allow the air to circulate – otherwise the ingredients may start to decompose.

Fresh meat, provided it is marinated in a cool place in a non-corrosive open dish and is regularly basted, will keep for up to 10 days; fish, however, should not be kept for more than 2-3 days in a fridge, unless it is being pickled; and fruit and vegetables, once they are bottled in airtight jars, can last for years.

Basic marinades

The recipes on the following pages are for special marinades which are uniquely flavoured. There are, however, certain basic marinades which are quick to prepare and deliciously simple, and most effective in tenderizing and flavouring. I thought it would be worthwhile to include a few recipes. The quantities for the marinades are sufficient for 1-1½ pounds of meat or fish.

Yoghurt marinade (suitable for chicken and white fish)

¼ pint (⅔ cup) stabilized
 yoghurt (see page 19)
juice and grated rind of ½ lemon
1 teaspoon mixed herbs

1 clove garlic, crushed
salt and freshly ground pepper
 to taste

Mix all the ingredients together and spread over the chicken or fish. Marinate for at least 1 hour in a cool place and cook as required.

Tomato marinade (suitable for veal, pork or white fish)

¼ pint (⅔ cup) tomato juice
1 onion, grated
pinch of cinnamon

1 teaspoon basil
½ teaspoon Worcestershire sauce
salt and pepper to taste

Mix all the ingredients together and spread over the meat or fish. Marinate for about 2 hours in a cool place and cook as required.

Wine marinade (suitable for beef or lamb)

1 glass red wine
2 onions, sliced
1 clove garlic, crushed
1 teaspoon mixed herbs

1 bayleaf, crushed
2 tablespoons olive oil
salt and freshly ground black
* pepper to taste*

Mix all the ingredients together and pour over the meat. Leave to marinate in a cool place for about 2 hours and cook as required.

Lemon marinade (suitable for chicken and veal)

juice of 2 lemons
1 clove garlic, crushed
1 teaspoon lemon thyme

2 tablespoons olive oil
salt and freshly ground black
* pepper to taste*

Mix all the ingredients together and pour over the meat. Leave to marinate for about 2 hours in a cool place and cook as required.

Glossary of ingredients

Angelica A perennial herb which is suited to our mild climate. Its stem and leaves are used to flavour liqueurs and to sweeten stewed fruit.

Aniseed The seed of the herb anise, which has a pleasant liquorice taste and is used to flavour drinks, salads and bread.

Basil Sweet basil and bush basil are the best known varieties and they are both annual herbs. It is at its most pungent when used fresh.

Bayleaves One of the most common aromatics in cooking, bay-leaves can either be used fresh or dried.

Bouquet garni Means a 'bunch' or 'faggot' of herbs. The usual blend is 1 bayleaf tied in a piece of muslin with a sprig of marjoram, a sprig of thyme and 2-3 parsley stalks. The bouquet garni should be removed from the dish before it is served. They can either be bought made up or you can prepare your own.

Capers The unopened flower buds of the caper plant which are pickled in brine. They add a sharpness to marinades and sauces and are especially good with white fish or beef. Substitute: pickled nasturtium seeds.

Cardamoms Gathered from a perennial plant which originates in India, they are sold in either seed form or as whole pods which must be crushed to release the seeds. They add a strong, clean flavour to food and are frequently used in curries.

Cayenne pepper An extremely hot pepper which is an attractive red colour and is often used sparingly as a garnish.

Chilli Either used fresh or dried or in powdered form, they give a hot, pungent flavour which is well known to all lovers of Indian and Mexican food. Their seeds can be discarded for a milder taste.

Chives From the same family as the garlic, leek and onion, their thin green leaves are used in salads, soups and as a garnish. Substitute: sping onions.

Cinnamon The bark of the cinnamon tree, which grows chiefly in South India and Sri Lanka, is sold either in sticks or powdered form. Cinnamon is used to flavour curry powder or as a sugar substitute to sweeten various drinks and fruit.

Cloves The dried flower-buds of a tropical tree, they have a pungent taste which is much used as a flavouring, either whole or in powdered form.

Coconut milk Used in South-East Asian food, it is difficult to buy fresh in the West. A commercially prepared creamed coconut is a good substitute, or you can make your own by soaking desiccated (shredded) coconut in water (allow 4 ounces (1⅓ cups) of desiccated (shredded) coconut to ¼ pint (⅔ cup) of water). For a smooth cream the liquid should be pressed through a sieve.

Coriander The seeds are used either whole or ground into a powder in many an oriental dish. The fresh leaves are also frequently used in cooking or as a garnish and can be bought from a good oriental delicatessen. Substitute for coriander leaves: parsley.

Court-bouillon Used for poaching fish or vegetables, it can also be reduced to form the base of an accompanying sauce. The ingredients are:

1 carrot, sliced	6-8 peppercorns
1 leek, sliced	1 tablespoon wine vinegar
1 onion, stuck with cloves	1 glass dry white wine
1 bayleaf	1½ pints (3¾ cups) water
1 bouquet garni	salt to taste

Put all the ingredients in a pan. Bring it to the boil, cover and simmer for about 20-25 minutes. Allow to cool and strain before use.

Cultured buttermilk The by-product of churning cream to make butter which is then cultured to replace some of the bacteria lost during pasteurization. It makes a creamy textured liquid which is used in marinades and salad dressings. Substitute: smetana or yoghurt.

Dill A gentle annual herb which is often used in pickling. Either dill weed or dill seed can be used, but the latter has a much stronger taste than the former.

Fennel The best known varieites are sweet and Florence fennel. Eaten fresh, it makes a delicious salad, or the seeds and stalks can be dried and used as a flavouring with fish or vegetables.

Five-spice powder A Chinese blend of spices containing star anise, fennel seed, cloves, cinnamon and ginger, it is superb with pork and duck. As opinions seem to vary as to what proportions of each spice it should contain (and indeed different brands seem to contain different spices), I would advise against anyone attempting to make their own. It can be bought from any Chinese supermarket.

Garlic One of the best known flavourings, it should always be used fresh. The various garlic flakes, chippings and flavoured salts in no way act as an adequate substitute for the real thing. The cloves can either be crushed in a garlic press, or with the blunt edge of a knife, bruised with the back of a spoon, or finely chopped, according to the recipe.

Ghee Clarified butter which is frequently used in India as a cooking medium. The butter is slowly melted and then strained through a piece of muslin to remove the sediment. It can be stored in the fridge and used as required.

Ginger Grown in the tropics, the root or rhizome of the ginger plant is familiar to us all. Fresh ginger must be peeled and sliced or crushed before cooking. Green ginger, which comes from the younger tubers, is sold in tins preserved in brine and needs no peeling. Once it has been opened, it must be drained, covered in sherry and stored in the fridge.

Geola djawa A Javanese sugar, used in stewing fruit, which has a superb nutty flavour. Substitute: molasses.

Harissa A paste used in the Middle East to flavour stews and meat, it is a blend of red pepper, garlic, coriander, cumin and salt. Mixed with a little yoghurt, it makes a spicy marinade for beef or veal.

Hoisin sauce A sweet Chinese sauce which is made from soya beans, sugar, garlic, chillies and vinegar. Sold in bottles or tins from any Chinese supermarket, it gives a distinctive flavour to a marinade.

Honey Melted in water, honey is frequently used to lightly sweeten fish, meat or fruit.

Juniper berries The purple/black fruit of an evergreen bush, the berries are picked and dried before they are sold. They impart a rich, gamey taste and they are an important ingredient in many a European dish. They can either be used whole or lightly crushed with the back of a spoon.

Lemon Slices of lemon, lemon juice or lemon rind are added to a marinade to sharpen the flavour. Always use fresh lemons and squeeze the juice as and when it is needed, otherwise it will sour.

Lemon grass Grown in the tropics, it can only be bought dried or in powder form in the West. It has a refreshing subtle flavour and is used particularly in Malaysian food. Substitute: lemon.

Lime Sharper but sweeter than the lemon, limes are imported fresh from the tropics. Concentrated lime juice is usually artificially sweetened and should not be used instead. Substitute: lemon.

Mace The outer covering or shell of the nutmeg fruit, it is used to flavour marinades and sauces. Substitute: nutmeg.

Marjoram A perennial herb which is delicious in salad and as a subtle flavouring with certain meats. Marjoram, or sweet marjoram, as it is correctly known, can either be used fresh or dried.

Mint A well known herb, it has a refreshing, clean flavour which is instantly recognizable.

Mixed herbs Prepared jars of dried mixed herbs differ in their mixture but they usually contain rosemary, basil, marjoram and thyme.

Mustard Which mustard you use depends on personal preference

– from a strong English to a lighter flavoured herbal mustard like Moutarde de Meaux. It can be lightly spread over a piece of beef or pork or mixed with oil as a marinade. Mustard seeds can be roasted and then crushed to make an aromatic flavouring.

Nutmeg The hard nut is either sold ready ground or whole, in which case it is grated when required.

Oil An essential ingredient for many marinades, there are different flavours and qualities of oil. A virgin olive oil (oil from the first pressing) is unbeatable for its taste; thick and an almost green colour, it is rich and nutty, but it is pure extravagance to use it all the time and not a very wise choice for those who are wary of their fat intake. A mixture of olive and vegetable oil is much lighter and cheaper and is usually sold as a blended oil. Sunflower, corn, sesame and pure vegetable oils all have distinctive flavours and can be used according to personal preference. I thought it worth noting that I recently discovered a new range of extracted volatile oils, available from good health food shops, to include such flavours as juniper, thyme, marjoram, orange and lemon balm. Presumably they can be used as flavourings, but whether they offer an advantage over the normal ingredient I am not quite convinced.

Orange-flower water Distilled from orange flowers, it is a lightly scented water which imparts a delicate flavour.

Oregano A perennial herb which is also known as wild marjoram. The Greeks, who cook with it liberally, use the flower heads, either fresh or dried; whereas the oregano which we buy in the shops is generally made up from the leaves.

Paprika Similar to cayenne or chilli powder, it is slightly sweeter in taste.

Parsley The most common of all herbs and one that we cannot do without. It provides a superb garnish and is used in many a marinade. It must always be used fresh as it does not dry at all successfully.

Pepper Black and white peppercorns are the same fruit but white peppercorns which is the milder version, has had the dark outer casing removed before it is dried. Traditionally black pepper is used with dark meats and white pepper with fish and white meats; but whichever one you use, always use it freshly ground. It is worthwhile investing in a good peppermill for that purpose. Peppercorns can be crushed in a pestle and mortar or with the back of a spoon. Green peppercorns are the unripe fruit preserved in brine.

Pickling spices A blend of spices used to pickle various meats, fish or vegetables. A good mixture will contain coriander, cassia, cardamom, chillies, bayleaf, mace, ginger, pepper, cloves and pimento. Unless you are very particular, it is much easier to buy a prepared blend.

Pomegranate seeds A sharp, sweet flavouring, the seed can be used fresh scooped out of a pomegranate, or bought dried in packets from an oriental delicatessen, in which case they may first need soaking in water.

Rosemary A well-known herb which is particularly delicious with lamb. Used either fresh or dried; because of its sharp pointed leaves, some people prefer to rub it (i.e. through a sieve) for a smoother textured dish.

Rose-water Distilled from rose petals, it is an exotic, sweet liquid which is excellent with certain fruits.

Rice wine Used in Chinese cooking, it adds a distinctive flavour to a marinade. Substitute: medium dry sherry or home-made version (see page 154).

Sage A much neglected herb, it has a distinctive taste which blends well with onions.

Salt Used in virtually every recipe, salt is an important and useful ingredient. Refined salt can be a little harsh and if added to a marinade, cause the meat to harden and toughen. Natural salt crystals, from either rock or sea salt, are a more gentle alternative and do have a superior taste. The crystals should be crushed when they are needed and this can be done by hand, in a pestle and mortar, or in a salt grinder. Spiced salt can be made up in advance, stored in an airtight jar and used as required. It is delicious with pork, but can be added to most dishes to give them a certain lift. The ingredients are:

8 ounces (1 cup) powdered salt
½ ounce (2 tablespoons) ground nutmeg
½ ounce (2 tablespoons) ground cloves
¼ ounce (1 tablespoon) ground white pepper
½ ounce (½ cup) mixed herbs, rubbed through a sieve
¼ ounce (¼ cup) bayleaves, finely crushed
pinch of cayenne pepper

Mix all the ingredients together and store in an airtight jar in a cool, dry place.

Sesame seed Generally sold in a raw state, the seeds should be roasted or dry fried before use.

Seville oranges In season during January and February, they are the bitter-sweet marmalade oranges. Their juice makes a unique marinade. Substitute: juice of 1 sweet orange and 1 lemon mixed together.

Smetana Naturally cultured milk, it has a sharp taste which is delicious as a dressing with potatoes. Substitute: buttermilk or soured cream.

Sorrel A refreshing perennial herb which is often added to sharpen the flavour of pates, or used in soups and salads. Almost impossible to buy, it is best to grow your own to ensure a constant supply.

Soy paste A heavily spiced paste made from fermented soya beans – also available from Chinese supermarkets.

Soy sauce A salty brown sauce made from soya beans which is an essential ingredient in Chinese cooking.

Star anise Similar to aniseed, it has a delicious woody flavour and can be bought from a Chinese supermarket. Substitute: aniseed.

Stock Often used instead of water as a liquid in cooking, the best stocks are generally home-made. Of course, you can always use a stock cube dissolved in boiling water, but once you get into the habit of making your own stocks, you will not want to change and they are an ideal way of using up bones and vegetable trimmings. As the stock is used in a variety of ways, it makes sense to add salt once the stock is made so it can be seasoned according to its usage. A basic chicken stock is:

1 chicken carcass and giblets	*4-5 parsley stalks*
1 large onion, chopped	*6-8 peppercorns*
2 carrots, sliced	*water to cover (1½ pints (3¾*
1 stick of celery and celery tops	*cups) approximately)*
1 bouquet garni	

Break up the carcass and place it with all the other ingredients in a stock-pot or saucepan. Bring it slowly to the boil and remove the scum with a metal skimmer. Cover and simmer for about 1½ hours. Strain through a sieve and set aside to cool. A fresh stock will keep in the fridge for about 3-5 days.

Note: Lemon peel, leek tops, mushrooms, tomato skins and garlic can also be added to the stock pot.

Tangerine peel Used frequently in Chinese recipes, you can either make your own by roasting it in a slow oven or buy it dried or in powdered form from a Chinese supermarket.

Tamarind Sold dried in pulp form, an infusion is made by soaking 2 ounces of the fruit in a little water for 1 hour. It is strained through a sieve or a piece of muslin and the acidulated, lightly flavoured water is then added to the recipe.

Tarragon A delicious liquorice flavoured annual herb, it has a striking flavour. Only French tarragon must be used; Russian tarragon, a bitter, woody perennial, is bitter in taste and has been known to ruin many a dish.

Thyme A savoury herb which has many varieties. Most common is garden thyme and other lesser known species are lemon thyme, variegated thyme and wild thyme. It can be used either fresh or dried and has a distinct country flavour.

Turmeric A brilliant yellow powder, turmeric is usually sold ready ground. It has a mellow flavour which is one of the basic tastes of a good Indian curry.

Vinegar Frequently used in marinades, there are many different varieties of commercially prepared vinegars including red and white wine vinegars, malt vinegar and cider vinegar. Malt vinegar is a little harsh and so I generally prefer to use a wine or cider vinegar. (See page 130 for flavoured vinegars).

Wine sediment paste Difficult to buy in the West, it makes an unusual marinade spread over chicken or duck. If you make rice wine use the sediment as a base for the paste with the following ingredients:

4 ounces (⅔ cup) rice wine sediment or
4 ounces (⅔ cup) ground rice
1 teaspoon sugar
6 tablespoons sherry

1-inch piece ginger, peeled and chopped
1 clove garlic, crushed
1 teaspoon tomato purée
2 tablespoons oil
pinch of 5-spice powder

Mix all the ingredients together and gently heat them in a saucepan until the mixture starts to thicken. Stir until it is almost dry, remove from the heat and leave to cool before use.

Yoghurt An important ingredient in Middle Eastern cooking, yoghurt makes a refreshing marinade. If it is to be cooked at a high temperature or added to a hot sauce, it is advisable to stabilize the yoghurt to prevent it from curdling or separating. This is simply done by gently heating 1 pint (2½ cups) of yoghurt and adding a lightly whipped egg white and a pinch of salt. Slowly bring it to the boil, stirring constantly, and then simmer over a very low heat for about 10 minutes. The stabilized yoghurt can be kept in the fridge and used as required.

Suppliers

Most of the herbs and spices can be bought from a good super-market or grocery shop; but for the more unusual ingredients, I have listed a few suppliers, all of whom will deal with mail order customers:

Baldwins Herbs
173 Walworth Road
London SE17

Culpeper Ltd
Hadstock Road
Linton
Cambridge CB1 6NJ
(mail order customers only)

Robert Jackson Ltd
170 Piccadilly
London W1

Bombay Emporium
70 Grafton Way
London W1

Cheong Leen Chinese
    Supermarket
4-10 Tower Street
London WC2

Borchelt Herb Gardens
474 Carriage Shop Road
East Falmouth, Mass 02536

Meadowbrook Herb Garden
Route 138
Wyoming, RI 02898

Rocky Hollow Herb Farm
Box 354
Sussex, NJ 07461

The Tool Shed Herb Farm
Salem Center
Purdy's Station
NY 10578

Yankee Peddler Herb Farm
Rte 4, Box 76
Highway 36N
Brenham, Texas 77833

Fish

FISH

As an island race, the English have enjoyed a long tradition of catching and eating fish. The Anglo-Saxons fished with the basket and the net and caught crabs, oysters, herrings, smelt and eels. Whale was also considered a gastronomic treat, it was brought to the table either roasted on the spit or boiled and sent in with peas. Apparently the tongue and tail were favourite parts.

It was not until the twelfth century that such familiar fish as salmon, trout, lobster, plaice, ray, turbot, sole and mackerel were identified and named in various manuscripts, and it is interesting to note how their names have remained constant over the centuries. Other fish such as lamprey 'of which our King John is saide to have been fond', bleak, limpet and grampus (sea wolf) have virtually disappeared from the fish stalls and markets; but as I have never eaten them, I cannot mourn their loss.

Fresh-water fish (with the exception of trout and salmon) are no longer a commercial proposition and are rarely seen on sale – but as Richard Dolby writes in his *Cook's Dictionary with a Plan of Ready Reference never hitherto attempted* (published 1830), 'There is often a muddy smell and taste attached to fresh-water fish' which is obviously none too pleasant. This taste can be eliminated by soaking the fish, after it has been cleaned, in a solution of salt and water, but generally I prefer sea-water fish.

With regard to buying fish, Richard Dolby is quite clear, 'There is a general rule in choosing most kinds of fish; if their gills are red, their eyes plump, and the whole fish stiff, they are good; if, on the contrary the gills are pale, the eyes sunk, and the fish flabby, they are stale.'

Always choose fresh fish for marinating. Gut and wash the fish under a cold running tap and pat it dry with a kitchen towel. The following recipes do actually state as to whether the fish should be filleted or left whole; whether you remove the head and tail is entirely a personal matter. I think that it gives the fish a more complete appearance to leave the head on, but then I suppose I am not very squeamish. I do remember serving a whole fish with stuffed olives inserted in the eye sockets and this so upset one of my guests, that she would not eat all the evening!

To ensure the marinade permeates thoroughly, score the fish diagonally on either side with a sharp knife. As a general rule fish should be marinated in a fridge and will keep for up to two days, although pickled fish will obviously keep a lot longer (see recipes for Herrings, Salmon and Mackerel). The time allowed for marinating will depend on the recipe and your schedule, although an hour is the minimum required. A simple recipe is to soak a prepared fish in lemon juice with a sprinkling of herbs – thyme and marjoram are especially good with fish – and a little freshly ground black pepper.

One last word – fish must never be overcooked as it loses its taste and texture. To test whether it is ready gently ease the fish from the bone with a sharp knife. If it is tender and falls away, it is cooked and can be served immediately.

SEA BREAM WITH OLIVES

serves 4-6

'My father was the keeper of the Eddystone Light,
Who slept with a mermaid one fine night,
And of that union there came three –
A porpoise, a porgy and the other was me . . .'
(from a folk-song)

Sea bream or porgy as it is known in North America is not to be confused with freshwater bream. The latter is an insipid fish, not particularly pleasant to eat, whereas sea bream has a firm, full flavour and when properly prepared, makes a satisfying meal.

1 whole sea bream, weighing 3-4 pounds

Marinade
2 cloves garlic   *grated juice and rind of 1 lemon*
1 teaspoon salt crystals   *¼ pint (⅔ cup) stabilized yoghurt*
1 teaspoon coriander seeds   *(see page 19)*
8 green olives, stoned and chopped freshly ground black pepper
 (or 8 coriander olives (see page
133) in place of the coriander
seeds and green olives)

Ask your fishmonger to scale the bream, as it is a tedious, messy business and he does have a special wire brush just for this purpose. Otherwise there is nothing for it and you will have to do it yourself at home with the blunt edge of a knife, pushing the scales in firm strokes in the direction of the head until they come away from the skin. If you cannot face the prospect of scales all over the kitchen floor and blocking up the sink – and believe me they are incredibly difficult to get rid of – you can always bake the fish whole and then carefully skin it before serving.

Gut and wash the fish and pat it dry with a kitchen towel. Make 3 deep incisions on either side of the fish with a sharp knife and lay it on one side on a large piece of aluminium cooking foil. Pound the garlic with the salt and coriander seeds (if used), and add the olives and lemon rine. Pour in the lemon juice and yoghurt and stir. You may prefer to use a blender, in which case you will get a much smoother paste.

Using a pastry brush, paint the marinade all over the outside of the bream, inside its cavity, and allow it to seep through the incisions. Sprinkle with freshly ground black pepper and wrap the foil loosely around the fish. Put it in the fridge and leave to marinate for a minimum of 2 hours. Bake the fish, wrapped in the foil, in a warm oven, 325°F, gas mark 3 until tender. Depending on the size of the fish it should take between 35 to 55 minutes. Serve immediately.

MARINATED HERRINGS

Sweden, with its innumerable lakes, rivers and long coastline, has always made good use of its abundant supply of fish. Best known to us are the recipes for 'sill' herring or 'stromming' Baltic herring. Usually the fish are salted before they are marinated and as I find the flavour of bought salted herrings a little harsh, I have included simple instructions for home salting. There are a variety of different ways of marinating the salted herrings and I have included a few suggestions.

Salt herrings

4-6 fresh herrings
1 bayleaf, crushed

1 pint (2½ cups) water
2 ounces (¼ cup) sea or rock salt

Clean and gut the herrings and carefully fillet them to remove all the bones (the skin can be left or removed according to personal taste). Arrange the fish in a flat dish and add the bayleaf. Dissolve the salt in the water and pour over the fish, making sure that they are completely covered by the brine. Leave to soak for about 3 hours. Drain thoroughy before use.

ROLLMOPS

serves 4-6

4-6 salt herring fillets

Marinade
*1 teaspoon of black & white   ½ pint (1 ¼ cups) white vinegar
  peppercorns, crushed   ½ pint (1¼ cups) water
1 onion, finely chopped   2 tablespoons sugar
1 teaspoon chopped dill   1 teaspoon tomato purée*

Mix the peppercorns with the onion and dill. Spread this mixture over each fillet, roll up and secure with a wooden toothpick. Bring the vinegar and water to the boil, add the sugar and tomato purée and stir until dissolved. Pour over the rolled herrings and leave in a cool place for about 24 hours before serving.

SOUR CREAM HERRINGS

serves 4-6

4-6 salt herring fillets

Marinade
*½ pint (1¼ cups) sour cream   1 apple, finely grated
juice of ½ lemon   freshly ground black pepper
1 teaspoon freshly chopped chives*

Mix the sour cream with the lemon juice. Add the chives, grated apple and pepper and pour over the salt herrings. Leave for a minimum of 8 hours before serving.

DRESSED HERRINGS

serves 4-6

4-6 salt herring fillets

Marinade
½ pint (1¼ cups) olive oil
1 onion, finely chopped
1 bayleaf, crushed

1 teaspoon English mustard
juice of 1 lemon

chopped dill weed and freshly ground black pepper to garnish

Mix all the ingredients together and pour over the herrings. Leave for a minimum of 8 hours before serving, garnished with the dill weed and black pepper.

SPICED HERRINGS

4-6 servings

4-6 salt herring fillets

Marinade
2 tablespoons sugar
¼ pint (⅔ cup) vinegar
¼ pint (⅔ cup) water

1 bayleaf
2 dried chillies
1 teaspoon pickling spices

Heat the sugar in the vinegar and water until it is dissolved. Add the bayleaf, chillies and pickling spices. Arrange the salt herrings in a glass jar and pour over the hot marinade. Seal the jar and leave in a cool place for about 4 days before serving.

FISH KEBABS

serves 6

Fish kebabs can be made from a variety of fish. The essential thing to remember is that the texture must be firm and meaty, otherwise the fish will flake or fall apart while cooking. Swordfish is ideal for kebabs but sadly is difficult to obtain, so I often buy fresh tunny fish or dogfish instead. Octopus and squid can also be used, either on their own or mixed with other fish, but they must be lightly boiled and left to cool before being added to the marinade. In the case of octopus, it is advisable to bash it thoroughly with a wooden meat hammer, unless you want to end up with unchewable rubber!

1½ pounds swordfish, fresh tunny fish or dogfish; or cooked octopus or cooked squid

Marinade
1 onion, finely chopped   *juice and grated rind of 1 lemon*
2 cloves garlic, crushed   *30 bayleaves, fresh or dried*
3 tablespoons olive oil   *salt to taste*

Prepare the fish by skinning and filleting it and cut it into 1-inch cubes. If using octopus or squid, cut the cooked flesh into convenient sized pieces for threading on to a kebab skewer. Put the cubed fish into a bowl.

Mix the ingredients for the marinade together and pour over the fish. If you use fresh bayleaves add them to the marinade, otherwise soak the dried leaves in boiling water for about 1 hour first, to allow them to soften. Leave the ingredients to marinate for about 3 hours in a cool place. Thread the fish on to a kebab stick, alternating each piece with a bayleaf. Brush over the marinade and cook over a glowing charcoal fire or under a pre-heated grill for about 10 minutes, turning the kebab sticks occasionally. To prevent the fish from burning, paint with the marinade while cooking.

NICO'S SALMON WITH GREEN PEPPERCORNS

serves 4-6

Nico Landanis is fast establishing a reputation for being one of the most inventive cooks in London. His restaurant, Chez Nico, is tucked away in the backstreets of Dulwich, which, under his supervision, maintains a high standard for original food. His style of cooking is based on a subtle blend of interesting and unusual flavours and this recipe is a departure from the Scandanavian Gravalax – salmon pickled in a traditional mixture of salt, sugar and dill.

4 salmon steaks, ½-inch thick

Marinade
2 tablespoons green peppercorns, drained
2 tablespoons brown sugar
2 tablespoons white wine vinegar
2 tablespoons white wine
juice of 2 limes
¾ pint (2 cups) olive oil

Skin the salmon, remove the bone and cut into thin strips or 'aiguillettes'. Combine all the ingredients for the marinade and as M. Landanis advises, 'play around with the ingredients, balancing the flavours until you get the taste you like, for although I have given quantities, I consider them no more than a guide'. Pour half the marinade into a flat dish and arrange the salmon on top. Add the remainder of the marinade, making sure that the fish is well covered. Place the dish in the fridge and leave the salmon to mature for 3-4 days, basting occasionally. Serve as a first course with cucumber salad (see page 126).

Note: I have tried this recipe using the exact quantities as stated by Nico and found it to be perfectly balanced. There is, however, a danger of adding too much lime juice, which gives the salmon an over-sharp flavour.

SPICED MACKEREL

serves 6

Oily in texture, mackerel is often passed over in favour of lighter and more subtle – and more expensive – fish. Yet, cooked with care, mackerel can taste quite delicious and are still extremely good value.

4-6 mackerel

Marinade
1 teaspoon pickling spices	*1 large onion, sliced*
2 dried chillies	*½ pint (1¼ cups) court-bouillon*
1 bayleaf, crushed	*(see page 12)*
1 teaspoon rock salt	*juice of 1 lemon*
freshly ground black pepper	*1 glass white wine (optional)*

6 lemon slices to garnish

Either choose small mackerel, which should be cleaned and gutted and cooked whole, or if you buy larger fish, do ask your fish-monger to skin and fillet them for you.

Arrange the fish in a shallow ovenproof dish. Sprinkle over the pickling spices, chillies, bayleaf, salt and pepper and place the sliced onion on top of the fish. Mix the court-bouillon with the lemon juice, and white wine if required, and pour over the fish. Cover with aluminium foil and bake in a slow oven, 300°F, gas mark 2 for about 1 hour, basting occcasionally. Allow slightly less time for filleted mackerel as you will find that they cook more quickly.

Decorate the fish with the lemon slices and leave to cool before placing in the fridge. Leave for about 24 hours before eating to allow the flavour of the spices to permeate.

SWEET AND SOUR FISH

serves 4-6

On their New Year's Day the Chinese serve carp as a symbol of endeavour, with a sweet and sour sauce to represent the rewards (sweet) and toil (sour) of the preceding year. The sauce adapts well to being cooked with grey mullet, bass or bream if carp is unavailable.

1 carp or grey mullet or seabass or sea bream, weighing 2-3 pounds
large pinch of rock salt

Marinade
2 teaspoons honey
1 tablespoon water
2 tablespoons soy sauce

2 tablespoons dry sherry or rice
* wine (see page 154)*
1 tablespoon vegetable oil
juice of ½ lemon

Garnish
3 spring onions, sliced
½-inch piece fresh ginger, peeled
* and sliced*

2 slices ham, cut into ½-inch
* strips*

Clean and gut the fish and rub it all over with the salt. Melt the honey with the water in a saucepan, and as soon as it forms a clear liquid, remove from the heat. Add the soy sauce, sherry or rice wine, oil and lemon juice and mix the ingredients together. Pour the marinade over the fish and leave to marinate for a minimum of 1 hour. When it is ready to be cooked, put the fish in a flat heat-proof dish with the marinade and scatter the spring onions, ginger and ham over as a garnish. Place the dish in a steamer and steam uncovered for about 20 minutes or until the fish is tender. Serve immediately.

Note: To improvise a steamer, balance a flat dish over a saucepan half-filled with water.

MUSSELS IN ORANGE AND BRANDY SAUCE

serves 4-6

Musselburgh in Scotland is named after the famous mussel bed found nearby at the mouth of the River Esk. Mussels were gathered there throughout the year, which casts a certain doubt over the old adage that shellfish should be eaten only when there is an 'r' in the month. Clams, cockles or scallops work equally well in this recipe.

4 pints mussels　　　　　　　　*1 bouquet garni*
1 onion, chopped　　　　　　　*¼ pint (⅔ cup) water*

Marinade
juice of 1 orange　　　　　　　*1 tablespoon brandy*

Garnish
4-6 slices bread　　　　　　　　*1 teaspoon chopped parsley*
2-3 tablespoons olive oil　　　　*grated rind of 1 orange*

To prepare the mussels, scrape their shells with a knife under a cold running tap to remove the barnacles and pull off their 'beards'. Discard any mussels with broken shells or with shells which will not close when given a sharp tap; these are dead and on no account should be eaten. Soak the mussels in cold water until required. In a large saucepan heat the water with the onion and bouquet garni until it is steaming. Add the mussels, cover and cook for about 5-7 minutes, shaking the pan occasionally. The mussels open as they cook. Remove from the heat and strain the liquid through a fine sieve and retain it. Remove the mussels from their shells and arrange in a shallow dish. Meanwhile reduce the strained liquor to about half its original quantity by boiling it vigorously and allow to cool. Add the brandy and orange juice and pour over the mussels. Leave to marinate in a cool place for about 8 hours.

Just before serving, fry the bread in a little olive oil to make croutons and cut into small pieces. Strain the mussels and serve with the croutons sprinkled over and decorated with the orange rind and parsley to provide a striking contrast in colour.

HONEYED TROUT

serves 6

One of the great surprises in taste is the combination of the sweet with the sour or savoury. The Chinese are famous for their various sweet and sour dishes, but less well known, although equally interesting, is the Moorish style of cooking. Originating from North Africa, the Moors had a love of luxury, opulence and good food. They cooked with fruits, spices, honey and wine, and developed a piquant taste which they introduced to the Spanish Peninsula when they conquered it in the Middle Ages. So strong was their influence that this dish has survived centuries of peasant cooking and is now accepted as truly Spanish in its derivation.

6 trout, weighing 6-8 ounces each

Marinade
2 onions, finely sliced
4 ounces (1 cup) mushrooms,
  finely sliced
1 teaspoon ground cumin
2 tablespoons honey

2 tablespoons water or court-
  bouillon (see page 12)
1 glass dry white wine
salt to taste

Gut and wash the fish in cold water and pat dry. Arrange the fish in a shallow ovenproof dish and scatter the onions, mushrooms and cumin on top. Heat the honey in a saucepan over a low heat with the water or court-bouillon until it has melted to form a clear liquid. Remove from the heat and stir in the wine and a little salt. Pour the marinade over the fish, cover and leave in a cool place for a minimum of 1 hour. Bake, covered, in a warm oven, 325°F, gas mark 3 until tender, about 25 minutes. Serve immediately.

See colour illustration facing page 40.

PLAICE IN ORANGE

serves 4-6

In France, the patisseries often use orange-flower water to lightly flavour and crispen their butter biscuits. They consider the finest water to come from the Brigarade or the bitter orange, as the sweet or edible orange-flower water is more cloying in taste.

1 white fish, weighing 2-3 pounds

Marinade

3 ounces (¾ cup) creamed or 4 ounces (1⅓ cups) desiccated (shredded) coconut
¼ pint (⅔ cup) hot water
2 cloves garlic, crushed
½-inch piece fresh ginger, peeled and crushed

2 fresh chillies, chopped
1 tablespoon chopped coriander leaves
pinch of salt
½ teaspoon chilli powder
½ teaspoon turmeric powder

Clean and gut the fish and with a sharp knife make three diagonal incisions on both sides of the fish. Soak the creamed or desiccated coconut in the hot water and leave to cool. Crush the garlic with the ginger, chillies, coriander leaves and salt to a smooth paste. Add the chilli and tumeric powder and stir in the cooled coconut water. Pour the marinade over the fish and leave in a cool place for about 8 hours. Cook either over a glowing charcoal fire or bake in a moderate oven, 350°F, gas mark 4 for about 35-40 minutes or until tender. Serve with a contrasting onion salad (see page 125).

COCONUT FISH

serves 4-6

In Kerala, a state in south-east India, coconuts and fresh fish are found in great profusion. The Keralites, who incidentally are a predominantly Christian race, grind the fresh coconuts squatting on their haunches with a sharp curved blade firmly grasped between their knees and extract the flesh with a rhythmical movement. I would suggest using either creamed or desiccated coconut soaked in water; it is less trouble and certainly a lot less dangerous. Pomfret, the fish which they cook, cannot be bought in the West. Instead I use any firm white fish, such as haddock, whiting, turbot or brill.

3-4 plaice (or lemon soles)　　　*6-8 anchovy fillets, cut in half*

Marinade
1 teaspoon mixed herbs　　　*1 tablespoon orange-flower water*
freshly ground black pepper　　　*1 glass dry white wine*
juice and grated rind of 2 Seville　　*1 ounce (2 tablespoons) butter*
*　oranges or 1 orange and 1*
*　lemon, mixed together*

lemon slices to garnish

Gut and skin the fish and fillet each fish into four. Lay each fillet flat and put an anchovy fillet on top. Sprinkle with the mixed herbs, freshly ground black pepper and grated orange peel. Roll up each fillet and secure, if necessary, with a wooden toothpick. Arrange the fish in shallow ovenproof dish. Mix the orange juice with the orange-flower water and white wine. Pour over the fish and add plenty of pepper. Cover and marinate for a minimum of 1 hour. Before cooking, dot the fish with butter and bake in a moderate oven, 350°F, gas mark 4 for about 20 minutes. Serve garnished with lemon slices.

Poultry

CHICKEN

The versatility of chicken is amazing. 'Fowls are to the kitchen what his canvas is to the painter, or to charlatans the cap of Fortunatus' wrote Brillant-Savarin, the French philosopher of food, in the eighteenth century. He considered the ways in which they could be served, 'boiled, roasted, fried, hot or cold, whole or in pieces, with or without sauce, boned, skinned or stuffed' and concluded that however they were prepared it was 'always with equal success', such was his love of chicken.

Another point in their favour was that the flesh was 'both light and savoury', and agrees equally with the convalescent and the man in the best of health. Chicken had a 'tender succulence which makes them worthy of our finest tables'; and Brillat-Savarin continued, 'who among us, after being condemned by a doctor to the diet of a desert father, has not revelled in a nice wing of chicken, the herald of his long-awaited return to social life?'

Chickens are, nowadays, one of the more economical buys for a family meal, due partly to demand and partly to what some people consider to be the scandalous practice of battery-rearing. It is interesting to note that this method of intensive farming is not new. In Brillat-Savarin's time chickens 'were condemned to martyrdom. Not only do we take away their means of reproduction, but we keep them in solitary confinement, cast them into darkness, force them to eat willy-nilly, and so blow them up to a size for which they were never intended'. A grim picture – but suffice to say that it did not put Brillat-Savarin off his chicken!

The argument against battery-reared chickens also revolves around the question of taste. There is no doubt that a free-range bird does taste better, but it is also more expensive and often difficult to buy. That is why marinating is important. It enables you to develop and enhance the flavour of what may otherwise prove to be a rather inspid bird. Any chicken can be marinated – free-range, battery reared, fresh or frozen and, with a subtle blend of ingredients, their flavour can only be improved. The chicken must always be thoroughly cleaned or prepared before it is marinated and it is a good idea to wipe it thoroughly with a kitchen cloth. In the case of frozen birds, always make sure that it is *thoroughly* defrosted and then wiped dry before the marinade is applied. Either whole birds or joints (wings, drumsticks or breasts) can be marinated and cooked, and although I have specified in the recipes what I consider should be used, they can always be adapted to suit your purposes. Keep your chicken while it is marinating in a cool place, either in the fridge or larder, and baste it occasionally if it is at all convenient, so that the flavour is evenly distributed. A final note; a defrosted frozen bird will generally take longer to cook than a fresh bird, so although I do state the cooking times for each recipe, they should be considered more as a rough than absolute guide.

CHINESE CHICKEN

serves 4-6

Drunken chicken is the ultimate in marinating with wine! A cooked chicken is left to soak for 2-3 days to absorb the delicate flavours. The taste will obviously depend on the wine, if possible do use Chinese rice wine (see page 154 for a home-made recipe) otherwise a pale sherry will make an admirable substitute.

1 chicken weighing 3-4 pounds

Marinade
2½ pints (6¼ cups) water
2 spring onions, chopped
2-inch piece fresh ginger, peeled and sliced

1 tablespoon salt
1 pint Chinese rice wine (see page 154) or dry sherry

Clean and wipe the chicken. Bring the water to the boil and add the onions, ginger and salt. Boil for about 5 minutes to release the flavours, then lower the chicken into the water. Cover and simmer for 15-20 minutes. Turn off the heat and leave the chicken to cool in the water. When it is quite cold, remove it from the saucepan. Drain, remove the skin and carve the chicken into small slices (for an authentic touch it can be sliced with a Chinese chopper or meat cleaver). Arrange the chicken pieces in a large jar and pour the rice wine or sherry over until it completely covers the chicken. Cover and leave to stand in a cool place for a minimum of 48 hours before serving. This makes an unusual first course and can be served arranged on a bed of bean sprouts in individual bowls.

CHICKEN IN CIDER WITH ALMONDS

serves 4-6

Almonds have been cultivated in Greece for centuries. Phyllis, according to Greek mythology, was changed by the gods into an almond tree after her lover, Demophoon, had left her. But Demophoon was stricken by grief and set out to find her. Eventually he came across a forlorn tree without leaves or flowers and, recognizing his lover, clasped the trunk to his chest. The tree suddenly burst into bloom. The almond has become the symbol of true love inextinguishable by death – hence the Greek tradition of serving sugared almonds at a wedding feast.

4 chicken portions

Marinade
1 teaspoon ground almonds   *½ pint (1¼ cups) dry cider*
salt and freshly ground pepper
  to taste

Sauce
2 ounces (¼ cup) butter   *pinch of ground cinnamon*
4 medium eating apples or 2   *4 tablespoons cream (optional)*
  large cooking apples, peeled,
  cored and chopped

1 ounce (¼ cup) flaked almonds to garnish

Wipe the chicken portions with a kitchen cloth and, using a sharp knife, make 1 or 2 deep incisions through the skin to allow the marinade to permeate. Mix the ground almonds with a little salt and pepper and rub the mixture all over the chicken. Place the portions in a flat dish and pour over the cider. Leave to marinate for about 6-8 hours, basting occasionally. When it is ready to be cooked, melt the butter in a heavy cast-iron casserole and brown the drained chicken on all sides. Add the apples and cinnamon and

pour over the marinade. Cover and simmer on a low heat for about 35 minutes until the chicken is quite tender, stirring occasionally to prevent the appples from sticking to the pan. Meanwhile toast the flaked almonds under a pre-heated grill until they turn a golden brown. Just before serving, stir in the cream if required and garnish with the toasted almonds.

DREDGED ROAST CHICKEN

'A good cook is as anxiously attentive to the appearance and colour of her roasts as a court beauty is to her complexion at a birthday ball' – Dr. Kitchiner, *Cooks Oracle* (mid-nineteenth century).

The Victorians 'dredged' their roasts in order to enhance their appearance and to season the meat. These dredgings or marinades were mixed together and then rubbed over the bird, which was left to stand and absorb the flavours. I have adapted Dr. Kitchiner's suggestions to suit our modern tastes. The recipes are suitable for a 3-4 pound chicken, which should be roasted in a fairly hot oven, 400°F, gas mark 6, for about 1 hour. Cover the breast with buttered paper to prevent it from drying, which can be removed about 10 minutes before the bird is cooked. Do baste the chicken – preferably with a bulb baster – as it will moisten the flesh as it cooks.

Herb and lemon dredge
1 teaspoon ground rosemary
1 teaspoon ground sage
1 tablespoon breadcrumbs

1 teaspoon grated lemon rind
juice of 1 lemon
salt and pepper to taste

Mix all the ingredients together and spread all over the chicken. Leave to stand for 1 hour before cooking. Dot with butter before placing in the oven.

Captions to preceding colour illustrations:
Honeyed Trout; An English country market; Spiced Indonesian Vegetables

Coriander and orange dredge

1 teaspoon coriander seeds,
  crushed
pinch of ground cinnamon
1 tablespoon breadcrumbs

1 teaspoon grated orange rind
juice of 1 orange
salt and pepper to taste

Mix all the ingredients together and spread over the chicken. Leave to stand for 1 hour before cooking. Dot with butter before placing in the oven.

Butter and brandy dredge

2 ounces (¼ cup) unsalted butter
1 clove garlic, crushed
1 tablespoon brandy

1 tablespoon breadcrumbs
salt and pepper to taste

Cream the butter and slowly add the remaining ingredients until they are mixed together (if the butter is very cold, it might help to warm it slightly but on no account should it be allowed to melt). Spread the mixture all over the bird and leave to stand for about 1 hour before cooking.

TANDOORI CHICKEN

serves 4-6

The Tandoori – a clay lined oven – originates from India and is a method of cooking introduced by the Moguls during their long reign over the sub-continent. The oven used to be made by hand and great care was taken in applying the clay; it was essential that it was completely smooth in order to conduct the heat. The clay imparted a unique flavour as the food cooked and turned it a deep rich red which is the recognized finish of Tandoori cooking.

An ordinary oven will work tolerably well for this recipe provided it is pre-heated before the chicken is placed in it: a few drops of cochineal or red food colouring can be added while basting the bird to give it an 'authentic' touch of colour.

1 chicken, weighing 3-4 pounds   *1 teaspoon rock salt*

Marinade
2 cloves garlic, crushed   *1 teaspoon ground coriander*
1 teaspoon chilli powder   *juice of 2 lemons*
1 teaspoon cumin powder   *¼ pint (⅔ cup) yoghurt*
1 teaspoon ground ginger   *freshly ground black pepper*

Garnish
3-4 drops cochineal or ½   *1 lettuce, shredded*
   teaspoon edible red colouring   *2 lemons, cut into quarters*
   (optional)

Clean and wipe the chicken dry. With a sharp knife remove the skin and trim away any excess fat. Rub the chicken with the salt and the discarded lemon skins, once their juice has been extracted, and leave for 30 minutes. Meanwhile mix the garlic with the spices and slowly stir in the lemon juice and yoghurt until all the ingredients are thoroughly combined. Paint the marinade both inside and outside the chicken – I find a pastry brush invaluable for this – and leave to marinate for a minimum of 5 hours. Pre-heat the oven to 450°F, gas mark 8 and place the chicken directly on the middle shelf with a baking tray on the bottom shelf to catch the fat. Cook for about 30 minutes, basting occasionally with the marinade. To prepare the colouring, mix it with the remaining marinade and paint it over the outside of the chicken. Cook the chicken for a further 10-15 minutes until it is really crisp. Serve garnished with chopped lettuce and the quarters of lemon, with a cooling raita as an accompanying salad (see page 126).

See colour illustration facing page 120.

CARIBBEAN CASSEROLE

serves 6

Caribbean dishes are derived from a variety of cultures. Elizabeth Lambert Ortiz explains in *The Complete Book of Caribbean Cookery* (M. Evans & Co. Inc. 1973, USA) 'In the Spanish-speaking islands, sofrito, a highly seasoned tomato-sweet pepper sauce, adapted from the original Spanish version, is widely used . . . dry or wet massala (curry powder or paste) and ghee (clarified butter) are used in Trinidad where the Indian influence is strong. An important Amerindian contribution is cassareep, a liquid seasoning made from grated cassava roots. Originally from Guyana on the South American mainland, its use has spread to Trinidad, to Barbados . . . and over to Jamaica in the Greater Antilles. A strong French influence can be seen in the use of seasonings . . . persisting when when the island ended up English.'

This recipe, taken from Miss Ortiz's book, which is published in the UK by Penguin as *Caribbean Cookery*, is Spanish in its origin:

6 chicken portions

Marinade
2 cloves garlic
large pinch oregano
2 teaspoons salt

freshly ground black pepper
2 tablespoons wine vinegar

4 tablespoons olive oil
1 onion, chopped
1 green pepper, seeded and chopped
2 tomatoes, peeled and chopped
1 bayleaf
4 ounces (½ cup) ham, chopped
1 tablespoon chopped parsley or coriander leaves

1½ pints (3¾ cups) chicken stock
12 ounces (1⅔ cups) rice, washed and drained
1 tablespoon capers
2 ounces (⅓ cup) stoned green olives, sliced
3 tablespoons sherry

Garnish
6 ounces (1 cup) green peas

2 ounces (½ cup) pimentos, sliced

Mix the ingredients for the marinade together and rub into the chicken pieces. Leave for about one hour. Heat the olive oil in a frying pan and saute the drained chicken until golden. Remove the chicken and add the onion and pepper and fry in the same oil until soft. Put the chicken pieces in a cast-iron casserole (see note) with the marinade, tomatoes, bayleaf, ham, parsley and about half the chicken stock. Cover and simmer over a low heat for 30 minutes. Strain the liquid to remove the chicken and measure the stock, adding the amount required to make the quantity up to 1½ pints (3¾ cups). Bring the stock to the boil and add the rice. Stir thoroughly and return the chicken to the pan with the capers and olives. Cover and simmer until the rice is cooked and all the liquid has been absorbed. Pour the sherry over and garnish with the peas and pimentos.

Note: If an earthenware casserole is used, a heat-diffusing mat must be placed between the dish and the source of heat – otherwise it is liable to crack.

CHICKEN SALAD

serves 4-6

'The salad – for which, like everybody else I ever met, he had a special recipe of his own' – De Maurier.

Nonetheless, I thought I would include my version! It is worth remembering to use a boiling fowl instead of a roaster for a salad. They are cheaper, provide plenty of moist flesh and, as it is marinated before serving – very flavoursome.

To cook a boiling fowl, place it in a large saucepan with enough water to cover. Add a large pinch of salt, a few peppercorns, a bay leaf, parsley stalks and some chopped vegetables (onions, carrots, leeks, celery or whatever you happen to have around). Slowly bring to the boil, cover and simmer until the chicken is tender. Remove from the pan, drain and leave to cool before attempting to skin and bone the bird. The liquid also makes an excellent stock and can be used as the base for a home-made soup.

1 pound cooked chicken, diced	*2 spring onions, sliced*
3-4 artichoke hearts, sliced	*1 teaspoon capers or pickled nasturtium seeds (see page 132)*

Dressing
2 hard-boiled eggs	*6 tablespoons olive oil*
1 clove garlic	*salt and pepper to taste*
2 tablespoons wine vinegar	

Garnish
1 lettuce, shredded	*½ cucumber, peeled and sliced*

Make the dressing by pressing the cooked egg yolk through a fine sieve into a mixing bowl. Then add the garlic and gradually stir in the vinegar to make a smooth paste and then add the olive oil, stirring continuously. Chop the egg whites and mix them in a separate bowl with the chicken, artichoke hearts, spring onions and capers. Pour over the dressing, add salt and pepper to taste and leave to marinate for about 2-3 hours. Serve arranged on a bed of shredded lettuce, decorated with cucumber slices.

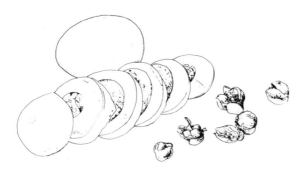

CUMIN CHICKEN WITH AUBERGINE (EGG-PLANT)

serves 4-6

The flavour of a stuffed chicken is superb. The secret is to stuff both the cavity as you would ordinarily, and also between the skin and flesh. All sorts of flavours are possible; minced mushrooms mixed with herb butter, cream cheese pounded with garlic, or chopped dried fruit and nuts soaked in a little wine – so do experiment! This recipe is adapted from an old Middle-Eastern cookery book, which was kindly translated by an enthusiastic friend.

1 plump chicken, weighing 3-4 pounds

Marinade
2 teaspoons cumin powder　　　*2 large aubergines (egg-plants)*
salt and pepper to taste

Wipe the chicken both inside and out with a kitchen cloth and carefully work the skin over the breast free, by sliding your fingers between the flesh and the skin, taking care not to tear it. Rub the cavity and under and on top of the skin with 1 teaspoon of the cumin powder and leave to marinate for a minimum of 1 hour.

To prepare the aubergines (egg-plants), slice them thinly, sprinkle with salt and leave them to stand in a colander for about an hour with a weight on top so that their bitter juices drain away. Wash and pat dry and sprinkle with the remaining cumin. Carefully slide the slices over the breast and pat them so they spread evenly. Stuff the remaining slices into the cavity and secure the skin with poultry pins so that the juices will not escape. Cover the breast with a sheet of buttered paper and roast in a fairly hot oven, 400°F, gas mark 6 for about 1 hour, removing the buttered paper for the last 10 minutes to allow the breast to brown. Serve immediately with a good gravy made from the juices.

CHICKEN SPICED WITH GREEN GINGER

serves 4-6

One of the pleasures of visiting Gerrard Street (London's Chinatown) is to wander around the Chinese supermarkets. A confusion of delicacies reigns, indecipherably labelled; florid mushrooms, strands of rubbery seaweed, mouth-sized sugar plums and tins of green ginger. More pungent and cleaner tasting than fresh ginger, the young or green roots are an essential ingredient to many Indian and Far-Eastern dishes. It is preserved, like green peppercorns, in brine. Once the tin is opened the ginger should be strained and submerged in sherry if it is to be kept for further use.

1 chicken, weighing 2½-3½ pounds

Marinade
2-inch piece green ginger
2 teaspoons coriander seeds,
  crushed
1 teaspoon salt
1 teaspoon black peppercorns,
  crushed

½ teaspoon cloves, crushed
3 cardamom pods, crushed and
  seeds extracted
4 ounces (½ cup) butter

Clean the chicken and wipe dry with a kitchen cloth and with a sharp knife make a few criss-cross incisions over the breast, legs and wings. Pound the ginger in a pestle and mortar – or you can do this in an electric blender if preferred – with the coriander, salt, peppercorns, cloves and cardamoms until they are thoroughly crushed. Cream the butter in a mixing bowl until soft and add the spices. Continue beating to mix the ingredients together to form a smooth paste. Fill the incisions with the spiced butter and rub the remainder inside the chicken and all over its skin. Leave the bird to stand for about 2 hours before cooking.

Either bake the chicken in a chicken brick or clay pot which has been soaked in water for 15 minutes, in the oven at 450°F, gas mark 8 for about 1 hour, or cook the bird, lightly wrapped in foil, in a moderate oven, 350°F, gas mark 4 until tender. Either way, just before it is cooked, uncover the breast to allow it to brown. Serve with cooked rice with the chicken juices poured over as flavouring.

DEVILLED CHICKEN

serves 4-6

This is a milder westernized version of Chicken Spiced with Green Ginger. It is ideal for grilled or barbecued chicken, although the original recipe, written in 1890, recommends that the chicken should be broiled.

'The best parts of chicken for a devil are the wings and legs. Remove the skin, score the flesh deeply in several places and rub in a fiery mixture made of salt, pepper, cayenne, mustard, anchovy and butter. This business should be done overnight. Broil over a clear fire and serve the fowl hot on a napkin. No sauce is required. Time, 10-12 minutes to broil.'
Cassell's Dictionary of Cookery (published London, 1890)

LEMON CHICKEN WITH OREGANO

serves 4-6

The name oregano is derived from the Greek and means the 'joy (ganos) of the mountain (orus)'. It is a wild marjoram which still grows in Greece and last year, while in Crete, I gathered bunch after bunch to take home for my friends and family. Even as I cook with it now, the smell evokes memories of sun-bathed hills transformed by velvety golden light and the dust and heat of a much-loved distant country.

4-6 chicken breasts

Marinade
1 teaspoon oregano
1 clove garlic, crushed
juice of 1 lemon

1 glass dry white wine
salt and pepper to taste

Sauce
1 ounce (2 tablespoons) butter
1 tablespoon plain flour
½ pint (1¼ cups) chicken stock

¼ pint (⅔ cup) single cream or
* creamy milk*
2 egg yolks

Wipe the chicken breasts and carefully remove the skin and trim away the excess fat. Arrange them in a shallow ovenproof baking dish and sprinkle over the oregano. Mix the remaining ingredients for the marinade together and pour over the chicken breasts. Marinate in a cool place for a minimum of 2 hours. Cover the dish with aluminium foil and bake in a moderate oven, 350°F, gas mark 4 for about 35 minutes, basting occasionally.

Meanwhile to prepare the sauce, melt the butter and stir in the flour to make a roux. Add the chicken stock and slowly bring to the boil, stirring constantly. Remove from the heat and allow to cool slightly. Beat the egg yolks and cream in a mixing bowl to make a liaison and gradually add about half a cupful of the sauce to allow the eggs to cook slowly without curdling. Carefully add the liaison to the main bulk of the sauce and re-heat gently so that the sauce does not separate or curdle. When the chicken is cooked, arrange the breasts on a serving plate. Strain the cooking juices through a sieve and add to the sauce. Beat it thoroughly for a few seconds and pour over the chicken. Serve immediately with boiled rice or buttered new potatoes.

DUCK

Duck were once described as 'excessively greedy and by no means nice feeders', which might explain why they are such a fatty bird. Wild duck, however, is a much leaner bird but since it became very difficult to buy (unless of course you shoot it yourself), I have discounted it for the purposes of this book.

Most ducks on the market tend to be of a mixed breed and come frozen. Always choose a plump-breasted duck and allow about 4-5 pounds prepared weight to serve four people generously. If you do buy a frozen bird, make sure it is thoroughly de-frosted before it is marinated, and it should not be left too long before it is eaten, otherwise it will taste rancid. Although there are various schools of thought about how a duck should be cooked, I find that after it has been marinated, it is best left to roast or casserole slowly, so that all the flavours can merge and blend together to make a well-balanced taste.

SALTED DUCK

serves 4

One of the earliest recipes for Salt Duck appears in Lady Llandover's *Good Cookery* (published 1867) where the duck is rubbed with salt and left to stand for a few days. The Chinese have a similar recipe where a mixture of salt and 5-spice powder is used, but my favourite version comes from Denmark, where they salt the duck and then marinate it in honey. The result is a pungent duck, soft as butter, which literally falls away from its carcass.

1 plump duck, weighing approximately 5 pounds

4 ounces (½ cup) rock salt crystals

¼ ounce (½ tablespoon) saltpetre (see note)

Marinade
4 tablespoons honey
3 pints (7½ cups) water
5 bayleaves
8 juniper berries, crushed

1 onion, stuck with cloves
1 carrot, finely sliced
½ pint (1¼ cups) wine vinegar

If possible do use a fresh duck for this recipe, otherwise make sure that it is well and truly de-frosted and wiped dry before use. Wipe the duck with a kitchen towel and with a sharp knife make deep incisions all over its skin. Mix the salt and saltpetre together and rub it all over the duck, both inside and out, cramming it into the incisions. Meanwhile melt the honey in the water in an earthenware casserole and when it is dissolved, add the bayleaves, juniper berries, onion and carrot. Simmer the marinade for about 5 minutes, remove it from the heat and add the vinegar. Allow it to cool before submerging the duck in it. Leave the duck to marinate for about 3-4 days in a cool place, making sure that it is completely covered in liquid.

Drain the duck and carefully skin it and remove the outer loose fat. This should only be done just before cooking, otherwise the flesh will harden. Either return the duck to the marinade (which gives it a sharper, saltier flavour) or place it in a casserole filled with fresh water. Bring it to the boil and cook it over a low heat until tender or bake it in a slow oven, 300°F, gas mark 2 for about 2 hours. Serve it either hot or cold with boiled rice.

Note: Saltpetre can be bought in small quantities from a dispensing chemist or drug store.

5-SPICED DUCK

serves 4

Chen-pi or dried tangerine peel is an important ingredient in Chinese cookery. It is especially good with duck and you can either buy it from a Chinese supermarket or make your own quite simply by drying it in a slow oven, 300°F, gas mark 2 for about 30 minutes and then storing it in an airtight container.

1 plump duck, weighing approximately 5-7 pounds

Marinade
1 teaspoon 5-spice powder   *1 tablespoon dried tangerine peel*
 (see page 13)   *2 cloves garlic, crushed*
4 tablespoons water   *2 tablespoons sherry*
4 tablespoons soy sauce

1 teaspoon cornflour   *salt and pepper to taste*

Wipe the duck with a kitchen towel and trim it to remove any loose fat. Prick the duck all over with a fork, rub the skin with the 5-spice powder and place it in a suitable dish for marinating. Heat the water with the soy sauce and tangerine peel and garlic and slowly bring it to the boil. Cover the saucepan and simmer for 5-10 minutes. Remove the pan from the heat and allow it to cool before adding the sherry. Pour the marinade over the duck and leave it in a cool place for about 2 hours, turning it occasionally.

Drain the duck and place it on a roasting rack over a roasting tin (a cake cooling tray can be used instead). Roast the duck in a warm oven, 325°F, gas mark 3 for about 1½-1¾ hours, basting it occasionaly with the marinade. When it is cooked, transfer it to a serving dish and keep it warm. To make the gravy, skim the fat from the juices in the pan, add any remaining marinade and stir in the cornflour. Slowly bring it to the boil stirring it continuously and then simmer it for 3-5 minutes. Adjust the seasoning and serve it separately with the duck.

CARRIER'S DUCK EN DAUBE

serves 4

Robert Carrier, cookery writer and restauranteur extraordinary, has a reputation for exotic, rich food. Here is his recipe for a tender duck.

1 plump duck, weighing approximately 5 pounds

Marinade
salt and freshly ground black pepper
1 celery stalk, chopped
2 carrots, sliced

2 large onions, sliced
8 tablespoons cognac
¾ pint (2 cups) dry red wine

4 ounces (½ cup) fat bacon, diced
1 tablespoon olive oil
1 bouquet garni

1 clove garlic
8 ounces (2 cups) mushrooms, sliced

Cut the duck into serving portions and place it in a suitable dish for marinating. Add the salt, freshly ground black pepper and the remaining ingredients for the marinade. Marinate it for at least 2 hours in a cool place.

Drain the duck and dry it with a kitchen towel, then set aside. Saute the bacon in the olive oil until golden, and remove from the pan. Brown the duck in the pan and then place it with the bacon and pan juices in a large cast-iron enamelled casserole. Cover and simmer gently for 20 minutes. Add the marinade to the pan with the bouquet garni, garlic and mushrooms, replace the cover and simmer over a very low heat for a further 1½ hours or until tender. Remove the bouquet garni, skim the fat, adjust the seasoning and serve immediately.

Meat

BEEF

'Any of us would kill a cow rather than not have beef.'
– Dr. Johnson

The Englishness of beef is indisputable. Roast beef and Yorkshire pudding was the Sunday joint, baron of beef 'two sirloins not cut asunder' was a cut much favoured by King Henry VIII and up until the last century, whole oxen were roasted over huge log fires to celebrate many a lord's birth, coming of age or wedding. Beef was highly praised by Mrs. Beeton as 'truly the king of the kitchen. Without it, no soup, no gravy; and its absence would produce almost a famine in the civilized world.'

A refrain from an old patriotic song reflects the popularity and, indeed, the importance of beef:

'O the roast beef of old England,
And O the old English roast beef'

It was sung at the expense of the French who, it was supposed, ate nothing but fricasseed frogs and consequently lacked courage, strength and stamina. Incredible as it sounds, such notions were meant to help us win the Napoleonic wars!

The quality of beef, 'depends on various circumstance; such as the age, the sex, the breed of the animal, and also on the food upon which it has been raised' (Mrs. Beeton). It is a sad fact that although the British eat a vast amount of beef and still regard it with great pride as their national dish, Britain now has to rely on imports for a large proportion of the beef which she consumes. Implicit in that is a decline in the freshness and texture of the meat and a rise in the prices. Consequently the cuts have changed; topside, cheaper and more economical, has replaced sirloin or rib as the most popular joint, and more and more people are buying frying or chuck steak instead of rump or fillet steak. Price has become the predominant factor to most cooks at the expense of taste.

However, as I always say, a judicious marinade can rectify the situation.

MARINATED STEAKS I

serves 4

Frying steak, cut from the top rump, buttock or 'leg o' mutton' is much cheaper steak to buy than the better known rump or sirloin. Well marinated, it is very tender and can taste delicious, so I thought I would include a selection of my favourite recipes. Incidentally, they can also be used both with the cheaper chuck steak or with the above mentioned more expensive cuts.

4 frying steaks

Marinade
2 spring onions, chopped
½-inch piece root ginger,
 shredded
1 tablespoon soy sauce

1 tablespoon hoisin sauce
2 tablespoons sherry or rice wine
 (see page 154)
2 tablespoons olive oil

Trim the steaks to remove the excess fat and beat them thoroughly with a wooden steak hammer or, failing that, your bare fist. Arrange the steaks in a suitable dish for marinating. Mix all the ingredients for the marinade together and pour it over the steaks. Leave the steaks to marinate for about 4 hours in a cool place. Drain the steaks and set aside the marinade. Heat 1 tablespoon of the marinade in a frying pan and cook the steaks one at a time for about 2-4 minutes on each side, depending on how rare you like your meat, baste each with a little marinade if necessary. Serve immediately.

MARINATED STEAKS II

serves 4

4 frying steaks

Marinade
1 teaspoon green peppercorns,
  crushed
1 clove garlic, crushed
½ teaspoon salt

2 tablespoons olive oil
¼ pint (⅔ cup) single cream (half
  & half)
2 teaspoons brandy (optional)

Prepare the steaks as in the preceding recipe. Spread the green peppercorns on both sides of the steaks and lay them flat in a suitable dish. Mix the garlic with the salt and oil and pour over the meat. Leave to marinate for a minimum of 4 hours, longer if possible, for a really pungent flavour.

    Drain the steaks, retaining the marinade, and scrape off any peppercorns which may be adhering to the meat. Heat the marinade with the peppercorns in a frying pan and fry the steaks one at a time for about 2-4 minutes on each side. Arrange the steaks on a dish and quickly heat the meat's juices to bubbling point. Remove from the heat, stir in the cream and brandy if required, and return to the heat for a further minute. Pour the sauce over the steaks and serve immediately.

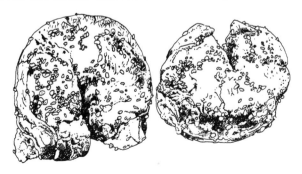

MARINATED STEAKS III

serves 4

4 frying steaks

Marinade
2 tablespoons sesame seeds
1 teaspoon sugar
1 clove garlic, crushed

2 tablespoons rice wine (see page 154)
2 tablespoons soy sauce

2 tablespoons vegetable oil

Prepare the steaks as directed in recipe I. Heat the sesame seeds in a dry frying pan until they begin to jump, then pound them in a pestle and mortar to make a smooth paste. Mix with the sugar and garlic and stir in the rice wine and soy sauce. Spread the mixture over the steaks and leave to marinate for a minimum of 4 hours in a cool place.

Heat a little of the oil in a frying pan and cook the steaks individually in their marinade, adding oil as required, according to the times suggested in recipe I.

MARINATED STEAKS IV

serves 4

4 frying steaks

Marinade
1 tablespoon good French mustard
1 clove garlic, crushed
1 teaspoon mixed herbs

1 teaspoon salt
freshly ground black pepper
2 tablespoons olive oil

Prepare the steaks as in recipe I. Arrange them in a suitable dish and spread each steak with a little of the mustard. Mix the garlic with the mixed herbs, salt, pepper and olive oil and pour it over the steaks. Marinate for a minimum of 4 hours, longer if possible. Drain the steaks, setting aside the marinade. Heat the marinade in a frying pan and cook the steaks according to the times suggested in recipe I.

Note: The steaks can also be grilled or cooked over a barbecue, in which case they should be basted with the marinade.

BRAISED BEEF WITH OLIVES

serves 4-6

Many Englishmen, and Mrs. Beeton in particular, believed that ragouts, daubes and estouffades were invented by the French to mask the poor quality of French beef. The French would never admit to this 'vulgar error' and their refusal to recognize the facts as seen by Mrs. Beeton was 'mere vaunting on the part of our neighbours, who seem to want la gloire in everything'.

2 pounds chuck steak

Marinade
1 teaspoon salt crystals
6-8 black peppercorns
1 teaspoon ground cloves
2 cloves garlic, crushed

1 teaspoon marjoram
3 bayleaves, crushed
1 onion, sliced into rings
1 glass red wine

1 tablespoon flour
3 tablespoons olive or
 vegetable oil
1 clove garlic

2 bay leaves
6-8 black olive, stoned and
 chopped (see note)
1 teaspoon freshly chopped parsley

Trim the meat to remove the fat and gristle and cut into pieces the size of small steaks. Crush the salt with the peppercorns in a pestle and mortar or with the back of a spoon and mix together with the ground cloves. Rub the mixture all over the pieces of steak and arrange the meat in a suitable dish for marinating. Add the garlic, marjoram and bayleaves, cover the meat with the onion rings and pour over the wine. Marinate the meat for a minimum of 6 hours at room temperature, or at least 8 hours if it is left in a cool place.

Drain the meat, reserving the marinade and scrape the meat to remove any herbs or onion which may be sticking to it. Sprinkle the meat with flour and set aside. Bring the marinade to the boil and let it simmer for a few minutes. Remove it from the heat and strain it. Heat the oil in a heavy based cast-iron casserole, add the garlic and bayleaves, and brown the meat on all sides in the oil. Pour in the strained marinade and bring it to the boil. Stir the stew gently, cover and simmer over a very low heat for about 2½-3 hours. It is advisable to place a heat diffusing mat between the casserole and the source of heat in order to control the temperature more effectively as the secret of the stew is to allow it to cook very slowly. About 20 minutes before it is cooked, add the olives and just before it is ready stir in the chopped parsley mixing it thoroughly with the gravy. Serve in the casserole dish with new potatoes.

Note: If you find the olives too salty, soak them in a little warm water for 10 minutes before use.

SPICED BEEF LOAF

serves 4-6

I first tasted meat cooked with harissa in Morocco. It is an oriental piquant flavouring blended from red pepper, garlic, coriander, cumin and salt, which, when used sparingly, is especially good with beef. Luckily I found that I can buy it in London at Robert Jackson Ltd, 170 Piccadilly, London W1, and they are also delighted to supply it on mail order.

2 pounds minced (ground) beef

Marinade
3 rashers streaky bacon   *1 teaspoon salt*
2 onions, grated   *freshly ground black pepper to taste*
1 teaspoon marjoram   *2 tablespoons red wine or port*
2 bayleaves, crushed   *2 teaspoons harissa paste*

Ask your butcher to mince the beef quite finely to make a smooth paste. This can be done by passing the mince through the mincer twice or by pounding it with a wooden steak hammer. Chop one rasher of bacon and put it with the mince in a large china or glass bowl. Add the onions, marjoram, bayleaves, salt and pepper and mix the ingredients thoroughly. In a separate bowl, mix the wine or port with the harissa and then pour it over the meat. Stir the mixture and leave to marinate for a minimum of 1 hour in a warm place.

Line a lightly oiled loaf tin with the remaining rashers of bacon and spoon the mixture into the tin. Cover the top with a sheet of greaseproof paper to prevent it from burning and bake in a slow oven, 330°F, gas mark 3 for about 1 hour or until it is cooked. Remove the greaseproof paper for the final 10 minutes to crispen the top. Either serve immediately, piping hot, or leave it to cool and serve with a salad.

BEEF IN BUTTERMILK

serves 4-6

The Austrians have an interesting marinade for a cheap cut of meat. They soak it in buttermilk, sharpened with capers and lemon rind and then bake it in a clay meat brick of clay pot.

3-4 pound piece of beef (any cheap cut will do)

Stuffing
1 onion, finely chopped　　　　　*1 teaspoon capers, chopped*
1 clove garlic, crushed　　　　　*1 teaspoon salt*
2 ounces (½ cup) mushrooms,
 finely chopped

Marinade
grated rind of 1 lemon　　　　　*freshly ground pepper to taste*
¼ pint (⅔ cup) buttermilk

1 teaspoon cornflour (cornstarch), optional

Trim the beef to remove any excess fat or gristle and lay it flat in a suitable dish for marinating. Mix the onions, garlic, mushrooms, capers and a little salt together and spread about two-thirds of the mixture over the beef. Roll and tie the meat to make a neat joint and spoon over the remainder of the savoury stuffing. Mix the lemon rind with the buttermilk and salt and pepper and pour it over the rolled beef. Leave it to marinate in a cool place for a minimum of 4 hours, basting it occasionally. To prepare the meat brick of clay pot, soak it in cold water for 15 minutes before cooking. Place the meat in the brick with the marinade, cover and bake in a fairly hot oven, 400°F, gas mark 6 for about 2½ hours, removing the lid for the last 20 minutes to allow the meat to brown. Remove the meat from the brick and carve into thin slices.

To prepare the gravy, skim the fat and slowly bring to the boil with the cornflour, (cornstarch), if required, to thicken it. Adjust the seasoning and pour over the beef and serve immediately.

Note: This dish can also be cooked in an ordinary earthenware casserole at 325°F, gas mark 2 for about 2 hours 45 minutes, but the beef should first be browned in 2 tablespoons of olive oil.

SAUERBRATEN – BEEF STEEPED IN VINEGAR

serves 4-6

'There is no better doctor than a good cook'. – German proverb

Sauerbraten is a traditional German dish, although I have found similar recipes in Corsican and early English cookery books. In all cases the pickle must first be boiled to extract the flavours and then left to cool before being poured over the meat.

3-4 pounds lean top rum of beef *pinch of salt*
1 clove garlic, finely sliced

Marinade
½ pint (1¼ cups) wine vinegar	*2 bayleaves, crushed*
¼ pint (⅔ cup) water	*½ teaspoon marjoram*
1 onion, stuck with cloves	*½ teaspoon thyme*
2 carrots, sliced	*2-3 parsley stalks*
2 leeks, sliced	*½ teaspoon salt*
1 clove garlic	*4-6 peppercorns, crushed*
2 tablespoons oil or pork lard	*½ teaspoon paprika*

Beat the beef with a wooden steak hammer and with a sharp knife insert thin slivers of garlic into the beef. Rub the meat with salt, roll and tie the meat and place in a suitable dish for marinating. To prepare the marinade, bring all the ingredients to the boil, cover the saucepan and simmer for about 10 minutes to release the flavours. Allow the marinade to cool and pour it over the beef. Leave to marinate for a minimum of 12 hours but preferably 3-4 days, basting or turning the meat in the pickle occasionally. Drain the meat and wipe it dry with a kitchen cloth. Strain the marinade to extract the vegetables. Heat the oil or lard in a casserole, add the paprika and let it cook for about 1 minute. Add the meat to the casserole and brown it on all sides. Add the vegetables and about one-third of the marinade, cover and simmer for about 2½ hours or until tender, adding more marinade if necessary. Remove the meat from the dish and serve with its cooked juices as a gravy.

BEEF ROLLED AS HARE

An old English recipe which I could not resist including:

'Take any piece of tender lean beef – inside of a sirloin to be preferred. Allow it to soak for twenty-four hours in a little port-wine and vinegar mixed, a glass of each. Make some forcemeat (see note), let it be very good, and place it with a slice or two of bacon on the beef. Roll and tie it, and roast before a clear fire, basting frequently with a sauce of portwine and vinegar, of equal quantities, and pounded allspice. Serve with a rich gravy, and send red-currant jelly to table with it. Probable coast for two pounds of meat 2s. 9d. (about 26 cents). Time, about three quarters of an hour.'

Note: 'Forcemeat of Beef – Take cold mashed potato, some slices of beef minced fine, a few savoury herbs pepper and salt. Mix these with two eggs to make a paste.'

SPICED BEEF (Good and wholesome)

serves 6-8 (see below)

The Victorians were extremely fond of spiced beef, partly because of its unique flavour and partly because it was a useful way of preserving meat as they had neither fridge nor freezer to rely on. My favourite recipe comes from Eliza Acton's book *Modern Cookery for Private Families*, written in 1845, but it is worth remembering that 'private families' were somewhat larger than they are nowadays, and it was not unusual for twelve to sit down to dinner. For more modest requirements, divide the quantities and time into half.

'Beef, 12 lb; sugar 7 oz (1 cup); mace and black pepper, each, 1 large teaspoonful; cloves, in powder, 2 large teaspoonfuls; nutmeg, 1; cayenne, ¼ teaspoonful: 3 days. Fine salt, ½ lb (1 cup); 12 days. Beef broth (or bouillon), 1½ pint (3¾ cups); onion, 1 small; bunch of herbs; carrots, 2 large or 4 small: stewed 4½ hours.

For twelve pounds of the round, rump, or thick flank of beef, take a large teaspoonful of freshly-pounded mace, and of ground black pepper, twice as much of cloves, one small nutmeg, and a quarter of a teaspoonful of cayenne, all in the finest powder. Mix them well with seven ounces (1 cup) of brown sugar, rub the beef with them and let it lie three days; add to it then half a pound (1 cup) of fine salt, and rub and turn it once in twenty-four hours for twelve days. Just wash, but do not soak it; skewer, or bind it into good form, put it into a stewpan or saucepan nearly of its size, pour to it a pint and a half (3¾ cups) of good beef broth, and when it begins to boil, take off the scum, and throw in one small onion, a moderate-sized faggot of thyme and parsley, and two large or four small carrots. Let it simmer quite softly for four hours and a half, and if not wanted to serve hot, leave it in its own liquor until it is nearly cold. This is an excellent and far more wholesome dish than the hard, bright-coloured beef which is cured with large quantities of salt and saltpetre; two or three ounces (½ cup) of juniper berries may be added to it with the spice, to heighten its flavour.

Observation: We give this recipe exactly as we have often had it used, but celery and turnips might be added to the gravy; and when the appearance of the meat is much considered, three-quarters of an ounce (1½ tablespoons) of saltpetre may be mixed with the spices; the beef may also be plainly boiled in water only, with a few vegetables, or baked in a deep pan with a little gravy. No meat must ever be left to cool in the stewpan or saucepan in which it is cooked, it must be lifted into a pan of its own depth, and the liquor poured upon it.'

BRAISED BEEF WITH STAR-ANISE

serves 6-8

In China, star-anise is often chewed after meals to promote digestion and sweeten the breath. Similar in flavour to anise, it is so called because of the grouping of its fruit to form an eight pointed star.

4 pounds braising beef or topside

Marinade
4 tablespoons soy sauce
1½ tablespoons hoisin sauce
6 tablespoons sherry or rice
 wine (see page 154)

1 tablespoon sugar
1 teaspoon salt
1 tablespoon vinegar
freshly ground pepper to taste

2 tablespoons flour
4 tablespoons vegetable oil
2 cloves garlic, crushed
1-inch piece fresh ginger, peeled
 and crushed

2 cloves star-anise
4 tablespoons water

Trim the meat to remove the excess fat and beat it with a wooden steak hammer. Prick it all over with a fork to allow the marinade to penetrate deeply and lay the meat in a suitable dish for marinating. Mix all the ingredients for the marinade together and pour it over the beef. Leave in a cool place to marinate for a minimum of 2 hours, basting it occasionally.

Drain the meat, setting aside the marinade, and coat it in the flour. Heat the oil and add the garlic, ginger and star-anise. Fry the spices for one minute, then add the beef and brown it on both sides. Mix the water with the marinade and pour a little over the beef. Turn the heat down, cover and leave the beef to cook very slowly over a low flame for about 1½ hours. A heat diffusing mat can be inserted between the saucepan and flame to control the temperature. Baste the meat occasionally, adding more of the diluted marinade when necessary to prevent the liquid from drying up. When cooked, remove the beef from the pan and cut into fine slices. Serve immediately.

– reproduced with kind permission of Mr. Kenneth Lo.

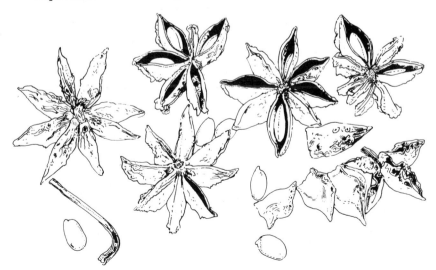

PORK

One of the earliest mentions of pork appears in the *Treatise on Utensils* by Alexander Neckham in the twelfth century. Writing for the aristocracy, Neckham advices on refinements which were beyond the reach of ordinary folk and suitable only to those who lived in the great castles. He gives minute directions for the preparation of various foods and mentions that the best way to cook pork was to broil it on the grill over a brisk fire to ensure that it was thoroughly and quickly cooked. He warned about the possible dangers of eating under-cooked or slowly cooked pork, and indeed his advice is still valid today.

Pork, a much maligned meat, was thought to be particularly liable to disease because of the pig's greedy habits. It had to be carefully cooked and in the pre-fridge days, people were advised to eat pork only between the cold months of November and February. Even today, the Jews and Muslims are forbidden to eat pork by their religious dietary laws as it was thought to be unclean. The standard or pork is much improved by the efficient methods of farming, the pigs are generally much healthier and all meat has to be tested to ensure that it reaches a high standard. Because the pigs are, in most cases, no longer able to feed wild, the meat does not have the same richness of taste, so what we have gained in hygiene, we have lost in taste.

A marinade can compensate for this loss of flavour and pork is the one meat which is ideally suited to a salt rub. Cassell's *Dictionary of Cookery* explains, 'All meats are not rendered equally salt or hard by exposure to the action of salt. Pork becomes less salt than beef'. Therefore because it becomes or absorbs less, it will not shrink or harden during cooking. The opportunities are tremendous for marinating pork; the Chinese have a long tradition of eating it highly spiced and I have adapted some of their recipes.

Do choose pork with care; the flesh should be pale pink, the fat white and firm and it should not give off any strong smell. Always marinate it in a cool place and never leave it in a warm room. It is still relatively cheap meat and one which, after a well-balanced marinade, will be tender and taste delicious.

MARINATED LOIN OF PORK

An old recipe which purports to be Germanic in origin. The sage can be substituted by thyme or mixed herbs to give the meat a more delicate flavour. Incidentally, the cost of a loin of pork at the time of writing this recipe was 9½d.-10½d. (old pence) per pound (about 2 cents a pound).

'Score a fresh loin of pork in the usual way and rub it well with powdered sage; lay the meat in a salting pan and pour over it two pints (5 cups) of tarragon vinegar and two pints (5 cups) of cold water; add 2 teaspoons of salt, one ounce and a half (¼ cup) of bruised peppercorns, a piece of garlic the size of a pea, twelve young sage leaves, and a small onion (see note). Turn and rub the pork everyday for three days. Take it up, drain it, rub it again with powdered sage, wrap it in an oiled paper, and roast before a clear fire. Baste liberally with the pickle. Serve on a hot dish, and send a sauce prepared as follows to table with the meat: – Mix smoothly in a saucepan two ounces (¼ cup) of butter and a tablespoon of flour; add gradually half a pint (1¼ cups) of the pickle with which the pork has been basted, a teaspoonful of moist sugar, half a teaspoonful of salt, a pinch of cayenne and a glass of port. Simmer the sauce over a gentle fire until it is of the consistency of cream and send it to table in a tureen. Time to roast, allow twenty-five minutes per pound' – Cassells, 1890.

Note: These quantities are for a loin of pork weighing approximately 6-8 pounds. For a smaller joint (3-4 pounds to serve 4-6 people) the stated quantities can be divided in half.

STUFFED PORK ROLL

serves 4-6

'How can a man die who has Sage in his garden?' – Arabian proverb

Sage, a much treasured herb, was called 'herb sacra' by the Romans and its medicinal uses ranged from a general tonic to a cure for snake bites. Its taste is particularly pleasant with pork and this recipe, which I devised for my book on fat free cooking (*Fine Flavoured Food*, Faber & Faber 1978), is much improved if left to marinate for a couple of hours.

1 boned loin of pork, weighing 3-4 pounds

Marinade
1 teaspoon salt
4-5 tomatoes, peeled and
 chopped
2 onions, finely chopped

2 cloves garlic, finely chopped
1 teaspoon sage
freshly ground black pepper

Sauce
2 tablespoons stabilized yoghurt (see page 19)

Ask your butcher to remove the skin and fat, while he is boning the loin, and to leave it unrolled. Lay the loin flat and rub it all over with the salt. Mix together the remaining ingredients for the marinade and spread about half of the quantity over the inside of the loin. Roll up the pork like a Swiss roll and tie it securely with string. Spoon a little of the marinade into a suitable dish, place the pork on top and cover with the remainder. Marinate at room temperature for about 1 hour or a little longer if in the fridge. Cover the meat with aluminium foil and bake in a moderate oven, 350°F, gas mark 4 for about 1-1½ hours. Remove from the oven, drain the meat, carve into thin slices and keep warm. Skim the gravy to remove the fat and strain through a sieve. Liquidize the tomatoes and onions with about 2 tablespoons of the gravy to make a thick puree and stir in the yoghurt. Heat the sauce in a double boiler and pour over the meat. Serve immediately.

Note: The meat can also be cooked in a meat brick or clay pot. The brick should be soaked for 15 minutes in cold water prior to use, and then the pork roll baked at 475°F, gas mark 9 for about 1¼ hours.

ROAST PORK RUBBED IN SALT

serves 4-6

'Salt is the policeman of taste; it keeps the various flavours of a dish in order and restrains the stronger from tyrannizing over the weaker.' – Chazal

1 leg of pork, weighing 3-4 pounds

Marinade
2 teaspoons spiced salt (see page 16)

2 tablespoons white wine

To prepare the leg of pork, remove the rind with a sharp knife and trim the fat to leave a thin covering layer. This, sadly, will mean that there is no crackling but the delicious flavour will more than compensate. Rub the salt all over the meat and leave it to stand in a cool place for a minimum of 12 hours. Before cooking wipe the joint to remove the marinade and dry thoroughly. Put the meat in a roasting tin and pour over the white wine. Roast in a slow oven, 325°F, gas mark 2 for about 2½-3 hours, basting occasionally. Serve immediately with a gravy made from the strained juices.

STEWED PORK IN BEER

serves 6

This recipe was kindly given to me by the German Food Centre in London. Obviously they advise using a German beer as their function in life is to promote their national products, but at the risk of offending them, I must add that any beer can be used instead.

2 pounds stewing pork, boned and cut into cubes

Marinade
2 onions, finely sliced   *freshly ground pepper to taste*
3 carrots, finely sliced   *1 bottle (about 12½ fluid ounces)*
2 cloves garlic, chopped   *beer*
1 teaspoon salt

2 tablespoons vegetable oil or   *1 teaspoon cornflour (cornstarch)*
dripping   *5 tablespoons water*

freshly chopped parsely to garnish

Put the prepared pork with the vegetables and the garlic in a suitable dish for marinating. Add the salt and pepper to taste and pour over the beer. Leave to marinate in a cool place for a minimum of 4 hours, longer if possible. Before cooking, strain the meat and vegetables and set aside the liquid. Heat the oil or dripping in a heavy-based, cast-iron casserole and add the drained meat and vegetables. Brown them in the fat until they are well sealed and pour in the beer. Bring to the boil, cover and simmer for about 1 hour, until the pork is tender. Mix the cornflour (cornstarch) with the water in a cup and add about 2 teaspoons of the gravy and stir vigorously to remove any lumps. Add the slaked cornflour (cornstarch) to the stew, stirring continuously until the gravy thickens. Simmer for a further 5 minutes. Garnish with parsley and serve immediately with boiled new potatoes.

Note: I have also tried this recipe adding a teaspoon of paprika powder to the marinade. I liked the extra pungency, although it may not be considered orthodox German cooking!

SPICED COLD PORK

serves 10-12

Elizabeth David's cookery books are a constant source of inspiration and delicious surprises. In *Spices, Salt and Aromatics in the English Kitchen (English Cooking, Ancient & Modern 1)*, Penguin Books 1970, Miss David explores the history of those ingredients related to English cookery and the result is an exciting reminder of long-forgotten delicacies which do much to re-establish all that is best about English food. I have taken this recipe from her book as it makes an unusual centrepiece for a cold buffet.

1 hand of pork, weighing 6 pounds

Marinade
10-12 juniper berries   *1 clove garlic*
1 tablespoon salt crystals   *2-3 bayleaves*
1 teaspoon black peppercorns   *4-6 dried fennel stalks*
4 white peppercorns   *½ lemon, cut into slices*

1 glass white wine   *water to cover*

1 tablespoon Madeira or sherry *squeeze of lemon juice*

A hand of pork – the fore-end of the shoulder and the trotter – is a 'buy of wonderful value'. As Miss David advises, ask your butcher to separate the trotter from the shoulder and to bone and remove the rind and loose fat from the shoulder to make a good joint. The butcher will roll and tie the joint and remember to ask for the trotter and trimmings.

Crush the juniper berries with the salt, peppercorns and garlic in a mortar with a pestle to make a thick paste. Rub the mixture all over the pork, pressing it into the meat as firmly as possible. Put the meat, skin side down, into a cooking pot (either an earthenware or an enamelled cast-iron casserole) with the trotter, bones and trimmings underneath. Add the bayleaves, fennel stalks and lemon slices and leave to marinate for a minimum of 2 hours, longer if convenient.

Pour in the wine and enough water to cover the meat and cook covered in a very slow oven, 300°F, gas mark 2 on the lowest shelf for about 3 hours. Remove the joint and leave it to cool. Continue cooking the bones etc. for a further hour to extract the gelatine. Strain the stock through a sieve and leave it to cool in a bowl. Once it is cooled, the fat will rise to the top to form a thick layer. This can be removed by skimming the jelly with a wooden spoon. Measure about ¾ pint (2 cups) of the stock and boil it vigorously to reduce it by one-third. Remove from the heat, stir in the Madeira or sherry and the lemon juice. Leave it to cool until it sets. Carve the pork into thin slices and serve with the jelly as a cold sauce.

Note: The remainder of the stock will make a delicious consomme.

5-SPICED PORK

serves 4

5-spice powder is an essential ingredient in many Chinese recipes. The variety I buy from Cheong Leen, the famous Chinese supermarket in Soho, consists of a mixture of ground star-anise, fennel seed, cloves, cinnamon and ginger, although I have noticed that it can contain cardamom. Typically, one brand of 5-spice powder is sold with a label listing a variety of seven spices – so it is quite difficult to find out exactly which spices it should contain. The flavour is unique and I find it makes an interesting combination of tastes with both pork or duck.

4 lean pork chops

Marinade
1 teaspoon salt	*1 teaspoon honey*
1 teaspoon 5-spice powder	*2 tablespoons white wine or water*
1 clove garlic, crushed	*juice and grated rind of 1 orange*

1 tablespoon vegetable oil   *2 onions, sliced*

Trim the chops and lightly score the meat with a sharp knife to allow the marinade to penetrate. Mix the salt with the 5-spice powder and the garlic to a smooth paste and rub it all over the meat. Heat the honey in a saucepan with the wine or water until it is melted. Allow it to cool slightly and add the orange juice. Arrange the chops in a shallow dish, sprinkle over the grated orange rind and pour over the cooled liquid. Marinate at room temperature for 1 hour, or longer if it is kept in the fridge, basting it occasionally. Heat the oil in a frying pan or wok (the Chinese rounded frying pan) and cook the onions until soft. Drain the chops and cook with the onions until browned on both sides. Pour over the marinade, cover the pan and simmer for about 10-15 minutes until tender. Serve immediately.

LACQUERED PORK CHOPS

serves 6

Tamarind (or imlee as it is called in India) is sold in blocks from most oriental groceries. It is soaked in water to make a bitter-sweet liquid which gives a refreshing tang to a sauce. Fresh pomegranate seeds are pulled from the fruit and either liquidized or pounded in a mortar to make a pulp. When the fruit is out of season, it is useful to know that oriental groceries also sell packets of dried seeds which can be stored and used throughout the year.

6 pork chops

Marinade
juice of 4 limes or 3 lemons   *1 teaspoon ground cinnamon*
½ teaspoon grated nutmeg   *1 teaspoon paprika*
½ teaspoon salt

Sauce
3 ounces tamarind   *8 ounces (1½ cups) soft plums,*
¼ pint (⅔ cup) water   *peeled and stoned*
2 ounces (½ cup) pounded pome-
  granate seeds (fresh or dried)

Trim the chops and lightly score the flesh with a sharp knife and arrange in a shallow dish. Mix all the ingredients for the marinade together and pour over the chops. Marinate the chops in a cool place for a minimum of 6 hours, turning them occasionally in the dish. To prepare the sauce, infuse the tamarind in the water for about 6 hours and then squeeze it dry. Discard the pulp and strain the water through a sieve. Heat the acidulated water in a saucepan and add the pomegranate seeds and the plums. Simmer over a very low heat until it forms the consistency of jam, stirring it occasionally to prevent it from burning or sticking to the bottom. Cook the chops under a pre-heated grill, basting them with the marinade to prevent them from drying out and remove from the heat. Spread a little of the sauce on both sides of the chops and return to the heat. Grill under a very hot grill until the sauce starts to caramelize. Serve immediately. – *Indian Cookery* (Penguin 1970) by Dhoranyit Singh.

RED STEAMED PORK

serves 6-8

This recipe comes from *The Chinese Cookery Encyclopaedia* (published by William Collins, 1974) by Kenneth Lo. Mr. Lo has done more than anyone to introduce Chinese cooking into our homes. His books are a fund of information both about the culture and food of China and are a pleasure to cook from.

3 pounds streaky belly of pork

Marinade
4 tablespoons soy sauce
1 tablespoon soy paste

4 tablespoons sherry or rice wine
  (see page 154)
1 tablespoon sugar

4 spring onion stalks, sliced

Cut the pork through the lean and fat into $1 \times 1\frac{1}{2} \times 2$-inch pieces, leaving a piece of skin attached to each slice. Mix the soy sauce with the soy paste, sherry or rice wine and sugar until well blended. Rub the pieces of pork with the mixture and leave to marinate for 2 hours.

Arrange the pork, skin side down, in a heat-proof dish. Pour in the remaining marinade and scatter the spring onions on top. Place the dish in a steamer and steam for $2\frac{1}{2}$ hours. Remove the spring onions and serve from the heat-proof dish.

LAMB

English spring lamb is renowned throughout the world. Its unique taste is due, as Mrs. Beeton wrote, to 'the damp climate, the broad pastures and the turnip crops that flourish under our rainy skies'. Mrs. Beeton was delightfully chauvinistic about English lamb and, while she grudgingly conceded that good meat could be found out of the British Isles, she declared that, 'the average is infinitely better in those Isles than anywhere else on the Continent of Europe'. The quality of English lamb, and indeed all our home-produced meat, has had a direct effect on our style of cooking. We 'have gained the habit of cooking meat so as to bring out the flavour and not to disguise it, while in other countries experience has taught to disguise it in many a cunning way.' In other words, plain English cooking.

Times have changed since Mrs. Beeton wrote her book in 1861. Nowadays we cannot produce enough lamb for our home market and over fifty per cent of the lamb consumed is imported from New Zealand. What we may have gained in cost and quantity, we have sadly lost in flavour; New Zealand lamb, although frozen under peak conditions, just does not taste as good. Thus the importance of marinating, although I think of it as enhancing and improving the meat rather than 'disguising it in a cunning way'.

New Zealand lamb is frozen almost immediately after it has been slaughtered – six hours delay was the time quoted to me by an official – so the meat is not conditioned or hung prior to shipping, with the result that it tends to be rather rubbery and tough to eat. A marinade, as I have said before, not only enhances the flavour of food but will tenderize the flesh and thus improve the texture.

Whether you buy English or New Zealand lamb, joint or chops, trim it well to remove the excess fat and then try one of the recipes on the following pages.

TARRAGON LAMB

serves 4-6

The use of tarragon with lamb is unusual but this original recipe of Glynn Christian's has a unique flavour; see page 83 for another of his recipes.

1 leg of lamb, weighing 3-4 pounds

Marinade

*3-4 sprigs of fresh tarragon
or 1 teaspoon dried tarragon
1 tablespoon oil
1 onion, sliced*

*½ pint (1¼ cups) dry white wine
salt and freshly ground pepper to
taste*

¼ pint (⅔ cup) cream

Skin the leg of lamb and trim away all the outside fat and as much of the fat lying between the muscle tissue that you can reach. Score the flesh deeply with a criss-cross pattern and stuff the slits with the tarragon. Rub the meat with the oil and cover with the onion. Place it in a suitable dish for marinating and pour over the white wine. Add a little salt and pepper and leave to marinate for about 2 hours in a cool place, basting occasionally. Roast the lamb with the marinade, basting it frequently, in a warm oven, 325°F, gas mark 3 for between 1 and 2 hours, depending on how pink you like your meat. About 10 minutes before the meat is cooked, pour off the marinade and meat juices into a saucepan. Reduce the gravy to half its original quantity by boiling vigorously. Carve the meat into thin slices and add the resulting juices to the marinade. Arrange the meat on a serving dish and keep warm. Remove the gravy from the heat, stir in the cream and carefully re-heat the sauce until it forms a medium-thick consistency. Pour the sauce over the lamb and keep warm.

LAMB TO TASTE LIKE VENISON

serves 4-6

Venison is expensive and at times difficult to buy and this recipe, a firm favourite with my friends, is a more than acceptable substitute. It does require a little organization; the lamb is marinated for 4-5 days at room temperature or 5-6 days in a fridge – so it must be bought well in advance of when you plan to eat it. It is not necessary to use the more costly fresh spring lamb, a lean New Zealand joint will do – and for the best results check with your butcher that the joint has been well hung.

1 leg of lamb weighing 3-4 pounds

Marinade
1 tablespoon oil	*3 bayleaves*
2 carrots, sliced	*8 juniper berries, crushed*
2 onions, sliced	*8 peppercorns, crushed*
2 celery stalks, sliced	*1 teaspoon salt*
2 cloves garlic, sliced	*1 pint (2½ cups) red wine*
1 teaspoon rosemary	*¼ pint (⅔ cup) wine vinegar*
4 sprigs parsley	

Trim the leg of lamb to remove all the loose fat and place in a suitable dish just large enough to hold it. Meanwhile heat the oil and slowly cook the carrots, onions, celery and garlic for about 5 minutes without allowing them to brown. Add the remainder of the ingredients and simmer slowly for a further 20 minutes. Remove the saucepan from the heat and leave to cool. Pour the cooled marinade over the lamb and keep it either in a cool place or in a fridge as stated above. Baste the meat occasionally – about 2-3 times a day – so that it is well and truly coated with the marinade and, after a while, you will see that the joint turns a pink-purple as it soaks up the flavours. Before cooking, drain the joint and put it in an oven-proof dish or roasting tin surrounded by the vegetables. Sear the lamb in a pre-heated oven 450°F, gas mark 8 for 15 minutes and then reduce the heat to 350°F, gas mark 4 and cook for a further hour, or until tender, basting occasionally with the marinade. Serve immediately.

LAMB OWAIRAKA

serves 4-6

Next door to our kitchen shop in London is Mr. Christian's, a delicatessen famous for its homemade pates, run by the energetic Glynn Christian, a fellow cookery writer. As a New Zealander, Glynn has been cooking lamb for years and has kindly contributed two of his favourite recipes, this one and Tarragon Lamb on page 81.

1 shoulder or loin of lamb, weighing 3-4 pounds

Marinade
1 teaspoon rubbed rosemary
¼ pint (⅔ cup) natural unsweetened apple juice
¼ pint (⅔ cup) fresh orange juice

salt and freshly ground pepper to taste
1 teaspoon lemon juice (optional)

With a sharp knife make an even criss-cross pattern over the lamb. Deepen 3 or 4 of the longest slits and stuff each one with the rosemary and place the lamb in a suitable dish for marinating. Mix the apple and orange juice together and pour it over the lamb. Marinate for a minimum of 2 hours, basting occasionally.

Cook the meat with the marinade, basting it, in a warm oven, 325°F, gas mark 3 for between 1 and 2 hours, depending on how pink you like your meat. The lamb must be cooked at a low temperature in order to avoid the marinade turning to caramel and ruining the flavour of the meat. When it is cooked, remove the meat and carve it. Skim the gravy to pour off the excess fat, adjust the flavour, adding the lemon juice if you find it a little sweet, and serve with the meat.

STUFFED BREAST OF LAMB

serves 4-6

'If the housekeeper is not very particular as to the precise joints to cook for dinner, there is oftentimes an opportunity for her to save as much money in her purchases of meat as will pay for the bread to eat with it.' – Mrs. Beeton on *How to Buy Meat Economically*.

2 breasts of lamb, boned

Marinade
1 teaspoon coriander powder   *pinch of ground ginger*

Stuffing
1 ounce (2 tablespoons) butter   *1 teaspoon chopped pistachios*
1 onion, chopped   *1 teaspoon chopped walnuts*
4 ounces (¾ cup) cooked rice   *1 teaspoon chopped almonds*
4 ounces (¾ cup) dried apricots,
 soaked overnight

Gravy
1 teaspoon flour   *vegetable or meat stock (as*
 required)

chopped fresh parsley or coriander leaves to garnish

Trim the breasts of lamb and lay them flat. Mix the coriander and ginger together and rub it all over the lamb. Leave it to absorb the flavours for a minimum of 1 hour at room temperature. To prepare the stuffing, melt the butter in a saucepan and fry the onions until transparent and stir in the remaining ingredients for the stuffing. Cook for a few minutes so that they are thoroughly mixed together, taking care that the rice does not burn, and remove from the heat. Spread this mixture on the inside of each of the breasts, roll them up, secure each one with string or meat skewers and place in an ovenproof dish. Sear in a pre-heated oven, 450°F, gas mark 7 for about 5-10 minutes and drain off the fat.

Turn down the oven to 350°F, gas mark 3 and cook for a further hour or until tender. Remove from the oven and drain off the fat and add the flour. Bring to the boil and add a little stock if the sauce is too thick. Carve the meat into slices, pour over the gravy and serve garnished with chopped parsley or coriander leaves.

ROAST GARLIC LAMB

serves 4-6

Lamb roasted 'à la francais' is seared in a hot oven to seal the flavour and then slowly roasted until the meat is medium rare, pink and moist. The lamb should be 'bien rassis' or well hung to be really tender, so if you have any doubts wrap the meat loosely and store it in the fridge for 3-5 days before cooking it, as suggested by Julia Child in *Mastering the Art of French Cooking*, Cassells 1963.

1 leg or shoulder of lamb, weighing 3-4 pounds

Marinade
3 sprigs fresh rosemary or   *3 cloves garlic, crushed*
  2 teaspoons rubbed rosemary

Trim off all but a very thin layer of fat and remove any loose fat. Pick off the leaves from the sprigs of rosemary and lightly bruise them in a pestle and mortar. Mix together with the garlic to form a paste. With the point of a sharp knife make deep incisions all over the joint and stuff each incision with a little of the paste until the lamb is studded with garlic and rosemary. Leave to marinate at room temperature for about 1 hour. Pre-heat the oven to 450°F, gas mark 8 and sear the joint for 15 minutes. Turn down the heat to 350°F, gas mark 4 and cook for about 50 minutes – 1 hour, depending on how well done you like your meat. Carve and serve immediately.

LAMB CURRY

serves 4-6

Indian 'Curry' was introduced to Europe in the seventeenth century, the earliest known recipe appears in a Portuguese cookery book *L'Arte de Cozinha*. Nowadays what we think of as 'curry' is no more than a pale imitation of the original dish; the subtleties of carefully blended spices are replaced by a teaspoon of curry powder and chopped apples and raisins mysteriously appear, owing their roots to I know not where! To try and rectify this, I have included a traditional recipe for Hyderabadi Masala Ghosh.

1½ pounds lean lamb

Marinade
½ pint (1¼ cups) yoghurt   *3 cloves*
1½-inch piece fresh ginger,   *1 teaspoon turmeric powder*
* peeled and crushed*   *½ teaspoon ground cinnamon*
6 peppercorns, crushed
2 cardamoms, crushed to extract
* seeds*

2 tablespoons ghee (see page 13)   *4 cloves garlic, crushed*
1 onion, sliced   *2 fresh chillies, chopped*

Trim the lamb to remove the gristle and fat and cut into 1-inch cubes. Wash the meat under a cold running tap, drain and dry thoroughly. Stir the yoghurt in a mixing bowl with a wooden spoon until it is quite smooth and gradually beat in the remaining ingredients for the marinade. Add the lamb and continue stirring until the meat is coated with the marinade. Leave in a cool place to marinate for the minimum of 1 hour. Heat the ghee in a saucepan until it is smoking and add the onion, garlic and chillies. Cook for about 2 minutes and then pour in the meat with the marinade. Stir briskly, cover the saucepan tightly and simmer over a low heat for about 40 minutes. Remove the lid and add a little more ghee if necessary to prevent the meat from burning and continue cooking until the meat turns a superb reddish brown. Serve immediately.

MARINATED LAMB CHOPS WITH BAYLEAVES

serves 4

The sweet bay or true laurel symbolizes success in herbal lore. The Ancient Greeks made crowns from the leaves to garland their heroes and poets – hence the derivation of our Poet Laureate.

4 lean lamb chops

Marinade
10 bayleaves   *1 glass white wine*
4-6 peppercorns, crushed   *1 tablespoon olive oil*
juice and grated rind of ½ lemon   *salt to taste*

Trim the lamb chops to remove the excess fat and place in a shallow dish. Combine the ingredients for the marinade and pour over the lamb. Leave in a cool place to marinate for a minimum of 6 hours, turning the chops occasionally so that they are thoroughly coated in the marinade. Fry the chops in a little of the marinade or drain and cook under a pre-heated grill or over a glowing charcoal fire until tender.

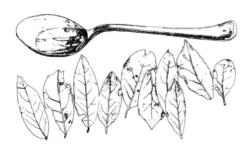

LAMB KEBABS

serves 6-8

The Arabs, even when they had ceased to wander the dry, arid deserts, 'remained nomadically prodigal with meat'. They ate lamb or mutton or kid (pork was impure and beef required too much of the precious pasture land), 'the tenderer parts cooked in slices or chunks (kebabs)'. Kebabs have become increasingly popular in the West and are ideal for barbecues or outdoor cooking, although they can, of course, be cooked under a gas or electric grill. – *Food in History* (Stein & Day 1973, Paladin Books 1975) by Reay Tannahill.

1-2 pounds lean, boned lamb (leg or shoulder)

Marinade (1)
2 cloves garlic, crushed   *juice of 1 lemon*
2 bayleaves, crushed   *3 tablespoons olive oil*
1 teaspoon oregano   *salt and pepper to taste*
juice of 1 onion (see note)

Marinade (2)
1 teaspoon ground coriander   *juice of 1 lemon*
1 teaspoon ground cumin   *salt and pepper to taste*
1 pint (2½ cups) yoghurt

Trim the lamb to remove most of the fat. Cut into 1-inch cubes and put into a dish or bowl. Mix the ingredients together for which-ever marinade you choose and pour it over the meat. Leave to marinate for a minimum of 1 hour – longer if convenient. (A Moroccan recipe states that the meat must be marinated for 12 hours before you even contemplate cooking it!) Drain the meat and thread it on to metal skewers or kebab sticks and cook over a glowing charcoal or wood fire or under a pre-heated gas or electric grill for about 7-10 minutes, depending on how rare you like your meat. Turn the kebabs as they cook so that they cook evenly, and paste them with the marinade to keep them really moist. Serve on a bed or rice or with pitta bread, which can be warmed as you cook the kebabs.

Note: To extract the juice from an onion, use a garlic press, a juice extractor or a liquidizer.

MARINATED LAMB CHOPS WITH MUSTARD

serves 4

'The seeds of mustard pounded with vinegar is an excellent sauce, good to be eaten with grosse meates, either fish or flesh, because it doth help digestion, warmeth the stomache and provoketh appetite'. – Gerard

4 lean lamb chops

Marinade
2 tablespoons mustard (Dijon,   *1 tablespoon tomato purée*
  Moutarde de Meaux or any   *1 clove garlic, crushed*
  herbal mustard)   *1 glass red wine*

Trim the chops and arrange in a shallow dish. Combine the mustard with the tomato purée and garlic and stir in the glass of wine. Spread the mixture evenly over both sides of the chops and marinate in a cool place for a minimum of 1 hour. Grill the meat under a pre-heated grill or cook over a glowing charcoal fire until tender.

VEAL

Best veal comes from a two to three month old calf and, at one time, when the whiteness of the flesh was all important, the butchers used to examine the insides of the mouth and the colour of the calf's eyes before buying, claiming that they could then judge whether the meat would be white or florid. As it is a young meat, it was thought to be rather indigestible and Dr. Graham, an eminent dietician of the last century wrote that 'it is so very an indigestible article, and has uniformly so strong a tendency to irritate the stomach and intestines, that I wholly proscribe its use whenever persons are not strong or healthy'.

Veal was primarily eaten as an entree, between the first course and the main meal, by the Victorians, whose appetites were somewhat more extended than ours. It was understandable, therefore, that the guests at a dinner given by a certain Scots nobleman were rather amazed to be served a dinner consisting of veal broth, a roasted fillet of veal, veal cutlets, a calf's head and calf's foot jelly. The host, oblivious to any lack of convention on his part merely explained, 'Aye, it's a cauf, when we kill a beast, we just eat up ae side, and doun the tither'.

Young veal has little fat and therefore needs to be carefully cooked to prevent it from becoming too dry. It can also be rather flavourless and so a marinade will perform the dual purpose of moistening and enhancing the meat.

GRILLED VEAL CHOPS IN LEMON

serves 4

'The principle of grilling is to cook the meat in such a way that it retains its richness, its flavour, its essential qualities. Therefore you bring it suddenly in contact with heat, you 'seize' it and close it so that nothing escapes. This you do on both sides of the meat: a good 'grillade' is slightly charred and fairly red inside. Grilling can also be done perfectly, even without a grill. All that is required is an ordinary iron pan like an omelette pan. Have it very clean, very dry and very hot. Dry your piece of meat in a cloth and simply put it in the pan dry. It will start grilling in the metal as well as if it were on a grill, browning nicely. Shake it occasionally. Do one side, then the other, a few minutes each side, according to your taste and the thickness of the meat'. – Marcel Boulestin, from an essay entitled *Pots and Pans* first published in *Wine and Food Magazine*.

4 veal chops

Marinade
2 ounces (½ cup) mushrooms,   *½ teaspoon thyme*
 finely chopped   *1 bayleaf, crushed*
1 onion, grated   *2 tablespoons olive oil*
juice and grated rind of 1 lemon   *salt and freshly ground black*
½ teaspoon chopped parsley   *pepper to taste*
½ teaspoon basil

4 slices of lemon to garnish

Trim the chops to remove the excess fat and lay them in a suitable dish for marinating. Mix all the ingredients for the marinade together and pour it over the veal. Marinate the meat for a minimum of 1 hour, basting or turning the chops occasionally in the marinade. Drain the meat and pat it dry carefully, so as not to remove the bits of the marinade which may have adhered to the meat. Cook under a pre-heated grill or, as Marcel Boulestin suggests, in an ordinary, dry, pan. Either way, baste the chops with a little of the marinade while they are cooking. Serve the chops garnished with a slice of lemon.

VEAL SYLVIE

serves 10-12

A delicious recipe which although it is reasonably complicated to prepare, is well worth the extra effort for a special dinner party. It comes from *Mastering the Art of French Cooking* (Cassells 1963) by Simone Beck, Louisette Bertholle and Julia Child, a book for which I have nothing but admiration.

5 pounds boneless roast of veal

Marinade
¼ pint (⅔ cup) brandy
¼ pint (⅔ cup) Madeira (see note)
2 tablespoons olive oil
2 carrots, sliced

1 onion, sliced
1 teaspoon salt
1 bouquet garni, (bayleaf, thyme and parsley sprigs)
6 peppercorns

Stuffing
6 or more slices of ham, thinly cut
12 or more slices of Swiss cheese, thinly cut
2 ounces (¾ cup) butter

1 tablespoon oil
salt and pepper to taste
2 rashers streaky bacon

Prepare the meat by making a series of deep parallel cuts 1-1½ inches apart, starting at the top and going with the grain the length of the meat from one end of the roast to the other, and to within ½ inch of the bottom of the roast. The pieces of meat will be free at the top and sides but should be attached at the bottom. Lay the meat carefully in a suitable bowl for marinating. Mix the ingredients for the marinade together and pour over the meat. Marinate the meat for a minimum of 6 hours or longer, basting it occasionally.

Scrape off the marinade ingredients and dry the meat, reserving the marinade. Lay the meat on a flat board, bottom downwards and cover each slice of meat with a layer of ham between two layers of cheese, leaving the outer sides of the roast uncovered. Tie the roast together with string and set aside. Strain the marinade and discard the bouquet garni. Heat the butter and oil in a large cast-iron casserole and add the vegetables from the marinade. Cook them gently until tender and add the veal to the casserole. Brown the base of the meat, basting the sides with the butter and oil. Place the meat uncovered in a pre-heated oven, 450°F, gas mark 8 and leave it to brown for about 15 minutes, basting it occasionally.

Meanwhile, boil the bacon rashers in water for about 10 minutes, rinse, drain and wipe them dry. Remove the casserole from the oven and turn the oven down to 325°F, gas mark 3. Add the marinade to the casserole and boil it vigorously to reduce its original quantity by one third. Season with salt and pepper, place the bacon over the meat and cover with aluminium foil. Cover the casserole and return to the oven. Cook it slowly, basting it occasionally for about 2½ hours until tender. Remove the meat from the oven and leave it to settle for a few minutes before carving it into crosswise slices so that each piece is covered with stuffing.

Note: I have also cooked this recipe substituing ½ pint (1¼ cups) medium dry white wine for the brandy and Madeira, which gives it a sharper flavour.

VEAL AND SPINACH PATE

serves 6

Spinach and sorrel make a superb base for a light pâté. In true French style, the pâté should be made in layers, the deep green of the leaf vegetables contrasting with the pale meat. It can be eaten either hot or cold and is delicious served with plenty of crusty French bread spread with garlic butter and heated in a warm oven.

1 pound lean veal
1 pound belly or neck of pork

1½ pounds fresh spinach
6-8 sorrel leaves (see note)

Marinade
1 clove garlic, crushed
6-8 peppercorns
½ teaspoon salt
pinch of ground mace

1 teaspoon thyme
1 bayleaf, crushed
2 tablespoons brandy
3-4 rashers streaky bacon, cut into small strips

Trim and chop the veal. Skin and bone the pork and trim away some of the fat. Mince it quite coarsely with the veal. Put the mixed meats in a mixing bowl and add the garlic. Crush the peppercorns with the salt and mace in a pestle and mortar and stir into the meat. Add the thyme and bayleaf, pour in the brandy and give the mixture a thorough stir. Marinate for about 2 hours in a cool place.

To cook the spinach and sorrel, wash them thoroughly and discard any of the stringy stalks. Put in a saucepan with just enough water to prevent them burning or sticking to the bottom of the pan. Cover and simmer over a gentle heat until they form a soft pulp. Strain through a sieve, pressing hard against the side with a wooden spoon or squeeze it between the palms of your hands to extract as much liquid as possible. The spinach and sorrel must be squeezed dry otherwise the pâté will be too moist and the texture will be spoilt. Roughly chop the leaves and season with a little salt.

Lightly oil a loaf tin or terrine dish and arrange the bacon on the bottom to line it. Spoon in a layer of the veal mixture about 1 inch deep, cover with a layer of spinach and sorrel and continue alternating the layers, finishing with the veal, until you have filled the terrine. Decorate the top with one or two bayleaves and spare pieces of bacon which you may have left over. Cover the top with a piece of lightly oiled greaseproof paper and place in a baking dish half-filled with water. Bake in a warm oven, 325°F, gas mark 3 for about 1 hour. Either serve it immediately or leave it to cool lightly weighted to press down the layers. Serve it straight from the terrine or carefully unmould it onto a plate to show it off!

Note: If you cannot find sorrel leaves, and I do find it is impossible to buy so I have to grow my own, substitute the juice of half a lime to sharpen the flavour of the spinach.

See colour illustration between pages 120 and 121.

VEAL IN ORANGE

serves 4-6

'Oranges, oranges,
Rich, flowing with juice,
Just arrived from abroad
Ripe and ready for use'
from *Cries of New York*, published 1830.

Peddlers have vanished from our streets. They were once a familiar sight hawking their goods, the streets resounding with their cries. Most famous of all street-sellers was Nell Gwynne, who sold her oranges in Covent Garden and later rose to become mistress to King Charles II.

1 leg of veal, weighing 2½-3½ pounds

Marinade

1 teaspoon tumeric	*freshly ground black pepper to taste*
1 teaspoon rosemary	*1 teaspoon honey*
grated rind and juice of 1 orange	*1 tablespoon water*
½ teaspoon salt	*1 glass white wine*

1 teaspoon cornflour

Trim the leg of veal and remove the skin, fat and gristle. Mix the tumeric with the rosemary, grated orange rind, salt and pepper and rub it all over the veal, pressing it hard into the meat. Put the veal into a suitable dish for marinating. Melt the honey in the water in a saucepan over a low flame. Add the white wine and half the quantity of the orange juice. Remove from the heat and allow it to cool before pouring over the veal. Marinate for a minimum of 4 hours in a cool place, basting it occasionally. Drain the veal and wipe it dry carefully so that you do not remove the herbs and flavouring which may be sticking to the meat. Wrap it in foil and roast in a slow oven, 300°F, gas mark 2 for about 2-2½ hours, basting it occasionally with the marinade.

When it is cooked, carefully undo the foil so that juices do not escape, place the meat on a warmed serving dish and pour the juices into a saucepan. Stir in the cornflour and slowly bring the gravy to the boil, stirring continuously until it starts to thicken. Add the remainder of the orange juice, adjust the seasoning and cook for a further minute. Serve immediately.

Note: The veal can also be cooked in a meat brick or clay pot. Prepare the brick or pot by soaking it in water for 15 minutes and place the veal with the marinade in it. Cover and cook in a fairly hot oven, 400°F, gas mark 6 for about 2 hours or until tender. There is no need to baste the meat when cooking in this way.

MARINATED BREAST OF VEAL

serves 2

'Take a breast of veal and cut it into pieces, and let it boil in some stock till three parts done; then take it out, and marinade it about an hour, with two spoonsful of vinegar, a little of the stock it was boiled in, some pepper and salt, two cloves of garlic, four of spices, sliced onions, thyme and bayleaf (see note); drain it, and fry it of a good colour with parsley'. – Richard Dolby *The Cook's Dictionary* 1830.

Note: So many of the earlier recipes are rather vague about the exact quantities required. My suggestion for the marinade is as follows:

1½ tablespoons vinegar
¼ pint (⅔ cup) veal stock
salt and pepper to taste
2 cloves garlic, crushed
pinch of ground mace
pinch of cinnamon

pinch of nutmeg
pinch of cloves or ½ teaspoon
  allspice
2 onions, sliced
½ teaspoon thyme
1 bay leaf

RABBIT

The best rabbit to eat was 'the sucking Rabbet taken in the nests' (*Twelve Months* 1661) and special breeding burrows were constructed to ensure that the Court had a regular supply of this delicacy. There is a theory that as these colonies grew, the rabbits could not be contained and so escaped to run wild in the country. It was not until they suffered myxomatosis quite recently that their numbers were in any way controlled.

As they became freely available, they were to be looked down on as a source of food by the upper classes and even today there still remains a certain snobbishness against the serving of rabbit. Yet rabbit makes an enjoyable meal and is still very good value, if a little on the bony side.

Both wild and commercially bred rabbits are on sale. The former has a stronger, more gamey taste while the latter, which tastes similar to chicken, is much more tender. Whichever you buy, make sure it is fresh as rabbit should not be hung for more than 36 hours. Ask your butcher to skin and joint the animal as it is a tedious business which he is much better equipped to perform.

Rabbit tends to be quite dry and should be marinated before cooking. Even if it is to be plainly roasted, soak it in a little flavoured milk or yoghurt before cooking to make sure the meat remains moist and succulent. A young rabbit should provide enough meat to serve 4 people; and do not forget that once it is eaten, the bones can be boiled up with a few vegetables and seasoning to make a wholesome soup.

COUNTRY RABBIT

serves 4

This is an old Romany recipe which was ideally suited to their open air life. The gypsies would kill, skin and joint a rabbit, gather the ingredients growing wild in the fields and cook it on the camp-fire. It is best suited to a young, fresh rabbit, but if this is unavailable, make sure that you marinate the rabbit for at least double the stated time.

1 rabbit, cut into joints

Marinade
4 ounces (1 cup) mushrooms,
  chopped
1 clove garlic, crushed
1 teaspoon chopped parsley
1 teaspoon chopped chives

4 juniper berries, crushed
2 tablespoons oil
1 tablespoon gin
salt and freshly ground black
  pepper to taste

Wipe the portions of rabbit with a kitchen towel and with a sharp knife make 1 or 2 incisions in each portion to enable the marinade to permeate more thoroughly. Arrange the joints in a shallow dish suitable for marinating and sprinkle over the mushrooms. Mix the remaining ingredients for the marinade together and pour it over the rabbit. Leave it in a cool place to marinate for about 2 hours, basting the meat occasionally.

Drain the rabbit carefully, so as not to shake off any bits of the marinade which may be sticking to it, and cook over an open wood or charcoal fire or under a pre-heated grill until tender. Turn the rabbit while it is cooking so that it browns evenly, and paint it with the marinade to prevent the meat from becoming too dry. Serve immediately with baked potatoes in their jackets.

SPANISH RABBIT

serves 4

1 rabbit, cut into joints

Marinade
2 cloves garlic, crushed   *4-6 peppercorns*
1 onion, sliced   *salt to taste*
½ teaspoon oregano   *2 glasses white wine*
½ teaspoon thyme

Sauce
2 tablespoons olive oil (see note)   *3 courgettes or zucchini, sliced*
1 bayleaf   *3 tomatoes, peeled and chopped*
2 rashers streaky bacon, chopped *1 teaspoon sugar or honey*
2 green peppers, sliced   *(optional)*

Wipe the portions of rabbit with a kitchen towel and arrange them in a suitable dish for marinating. Mix all the ingredients for the marinade together and pour it over the rabbit. Leave it in a cool place for about 4 hours, turning it occasionally.

Drain the joints, reserving the marinade, and wipe dry. Heat the olive oil in a cast-iron casserole and add the bayleaf and bacon. Cook for a few minutes and then remove from the pan. Add the drained joints of rabbit and brown them on all sides. Return the bacon and bayleaf to the casserole and pour over the marinade. Cover and simmer over a low heat for about 45 minutes, checking every so often that there is sufficient liquid in the pan. Add the peppers and courgettes or zucchini and simmer for another 15 minutes. Add the tomatoes, stir thoroughly and simmer for a further 15 minutes. Remove the lid and allow the sauce to reduce to a thick consistency. Taste it and add the sugar if required. Remove the bayleaf and serve immediately.

Note: This dish can be cooked with tomato juice instead of oil for a lower fat content version.

LIVER

Memories of liver come flooding back from my childhood, 'liver, ugh!' 'Eat it all up, otherwise you will never grow up big and strong', was the reply and, forced to swallow every mouthful, I soldiered on. Years later, when I rediscovered liver, it was to my amazement, quite delicious, ridiculously cheap and, as a further inducement, rich in trace elements and the vitamins A and B12. They must have been right after all!

Liver, which is classed as offal or variety meats, should be eaten as fresh as possible. Chicken liver is a good buy and so is lambs' liver, which is cheaper than calves' liver and just as tasty. As a general rule I avoid ox or pigs' liver (except in pates) as they are coarsely flavoured and textured and, although it does help if you soak them in milk before marinating, I do not think it is worth the effort.

Liver contains no fat and should be tenderized before cooking with a marinade. Unless carefully prepared and quickly cooked, it can be quite tough and dry so it is advisable to cut the liver into thin slices to allow the marinade to penetrate thoroughly (you can also prick it all over with a fork) and to enable it to be cooked as quickly as possible.

The marinades in the following recipes for liver will tenderize and flavour the meat, but I thought it useful to include a basic marinade which should be applied about 1 hour before cooking: For every pound of liver allow 1 tablespoon of vinegar to 2 tablespoons of oil, salt and pepper and any herbs can be added to taste.

LIVER WITH TARRAGON

serves 4-6

Estragon, the French for tarragon, means little dragon. It was so called as it was thought to be an effective cure for snake (little dragon) bites and also because of the bite or sting to its taste. As a word of warning, always cook with French as opposed to Russian tarragon. The latter tends to give a bitter, unpleasant taste to food and should never be confused with the former.

1½ pounds lambs' liver

Marinade
1 teaspoon tarragon　　　　　　　　*grated rind and juice of 1 lemon*
salt and freshly ground black
*　pepper to taste*

2 onions, finely sliced　　　　　*½ pint (1¼ cups) chicken stock or*
　　　　　　　　　　　　　　¼ pint (⅔ cup) stock and ¼ pint
　　　　　　　　　　　　　　(⅔ cup) white wine (see note)

Ask your butcher to cut the liver finely into thin slices. Wipe the slices with a kitchen towel and arrange them in a flat dish for marinating. Sprinkle over the tarragon, salt and pepper and the orange rind, pressing them into the meat. Pour over the orange juice and leave to marinate, turning occasionally, for about 1 hour. Heat a little of the stock in a heavy-based frying pan or casserole and sweat the onions until tender, adding more stock as required. Drain the liver, retaining the marinade, and add it to the pan. Cook it for about 5 minutes, depending on how rare you like it, over a gentle heat. Remove the liver and keep it warm. Pour in the remaining stock or wine and the marinade and bring it to the boil. Simmer the sauce for about 3 minutes, stirring it constantly, and then pour it over the meat. Serve immediately.

Note: Liver is an ideal meat to be cooked without any added fat or starch as the blood released from it as it cooks will make a rich, thick sauce. Stock, sufficiently heated, is an alternative medium for browning or sealing food and, if used instead of butter or oil, gives a lighter, cleaner taste.

CHICKEN LIVER PATE

serves 4-6

For a really good pâté, make it at least two days in advance: first marinating the ingredients, then once they are cooked, sealing the pâté with clarified butter and leaving it in a cool place to 'ripen'. The texture of the pâté is a matter of personal preference, I favour it really smooth so I usually liquidize the ingredients in an electric blender, but they can be pounded in a pestle and mortar or simply mashed with a fork.

8 ounces (1 cup) chicken livers

Marinade
1 clove garlic, crushed *1 bayleaf*
½ teaspoon thyme *1 glass red wine*
½ teaspoon rosemary *salt and freshly ground black*
4-6 juniper berries, crushed *pepper to taste*

1 onion, finely sliced *4 ounces (½ cup) butter*

3-4 bayleaves to garnish

Roughly chop the chicken livers and arrange them in a bowl. Add the garlic, thyme, rosemary, juniper berries and bayleaf, pour over the red wine and add the seasoning. Stir the ingredients together and leave them to marinate for a minimum of 1 hour.

Heat 2 ounces (¼ cup) of the butter in a frying pan and cook the onion until it turns a translucent golden brown. Drain the chicken livers, reserving the marinade, and add them to the onions. Cook over a gentle heat, slowly adding the marinade until the livers are brown on the outside but still quite pink on the inside and the butter and marinade have combined to form a rich, thick gravy. Remove the bayleaf and mash or liquidize the ingredients to form a rough or smooth paste (depending on your taste). Spoon the pâté into a suitable dish and leave it to cool slightly. To clarify the butter, melt the remaining 2 ounces (¼ cup) over a low heat to prevent it from browning. Strain it through a fine sieve lined with a piece of muslin to remove the impurities and allow it to cool slightly before pouring it over the pâté to seal it. Decorate the top with bayleaves and leave it for about 2 days before serving.

LIVER KEBABS

serves 4-6

Sis kebab comes from the Turkish *sis*, meaning sword or skewer, and *kebab*, meaning lamb or mutton. A kebab has come to mean virtually any kind of meat, be it chicken, beef, pork or even fish, which is cut into small pieces, threaded on to a skewer and grilled or cooked over an open fire until tender. This recipe comes from India, where *kababs*, as they are known there, were originally introduced by the Moghuls.

1½ pounds (3 cups) lambs' liver

Marinade
juice of 2 limes   *2 onions, finely minced*
2-inch piece green ginger, crushed   *2 tablespoons chopped parsley*
½ teaspoon salt crystals, crushed   *or coriander leaves*
8-10 black peppercorns, crushed   *2 tablespoons yoghurt*

Ask your butcher to cut the liver into 1-1½-inch thick slices. Wash it and pat it dry with a kitchen towel and rub each slice with the lime juice. Leave for 30 minutes. Mix the crushed spices to form a thick paste, this can be done very easily in a liquidizer or with a pestle and mortar, and stir in the yoghurt. Prick the slices of liver with a fork to enable the marinade to penetrate more deeply and cut into 1-1½-inch cubes. Put the cubes of liver in a bowl, add the lime to the marinade and spread it over the meat. Leave for about 3-4 hours in a cool place, turning the meat occasionally.

Thread the liver on to skewers and cook under a pre-heated grill or over a barbecue, turning and painting them with the marinade as they cook to prevent the meat from drying up. Serve immediately with rice or hot pitta bread and a fresh salad.

MIDDLE EASTERN LIVER

serves 4-6

As Claudia Roden points out in *A Book of Middle Eastern Food*, (Thomas Nelson, 1968), Muslims are forbidden to drink any alcohol and they often substitute vinegar for wine in their cooking. Actually, the vinegar gives an unusual sharpness which no wine could ever achieve.

1½ pounds (3 cups) lambs' liver

Marinade
½ teaspoon chilli powder
½ teaspoon sugar
*¼ pint (⅔ cup) chilli vinegar
  (see page 000) or wine vinegar*

2 tablespoons oil
*salt and freshly ground black
  pepper to taste*

2 tablespoons oil
2 tablespoons breadcrumbs

2 cloves garlic, crushed

freshly chopped parsley to garnish

Ask your butcher to slice the liver quite finely. Wash and pat it dry with a kitchen towel and rub the slices with the chilli powder. Arrange the meat in a flat dish. Dissolve the sugar in the vinegar and allow to cool before adding the oil and the salt and pepper. Pour the mixture over the liver and leave to marinate for about 1 hour in a cool place, basting it occasionally.

Heat 2 tablespoons of oil in a cast-iron casserole and cook the breadcrumbs and garlic until golden brown. Drain the meat and add the marinade to the casserole and bring it to the boil. Poach the liver in the mixture, simmering it gently for about 5-10 minutes. Serve with plenty of freshly chopped parsley to provide an interesting contrast of colours.

GAME

Game, which covers all wild animals hunted for food, must be hung to condition; otherwise, as one friend remarked, venison tastes like a tough piece of lamb and partridge is worse than a half-cooked chicken! As a rough guide allow 7 days for venison, 2-3 days for partridge and wood pigeon; but, of course, these times will vary with the weather as a muggy day will quicken the process, whereas a cold day will slow it down.

If you are buying game – as opposed to shooting it yourself – a good game purveyor will sell his meat already hung or at least will tell you how much longer it will need, and provided the meat is matured, he will pluck and clean it for you.

I must admit to baulking at the task of plucking and cleaning, no matter how careful I am I always cover the kitchen (and myself) in feathers, so I inevitably end by bribing the local butcher, who proudly boasts a game licence, to perform the task for me. Actually for a small sum most licensed butchers will do it for you, so you can save yourself the trouble.

Young birds are most suited to roasting, the older birds tend to be a little tough even after a long period of marinating and so should be braised or casseroled. Venison can be roasted, fried or casseroled, but needs careful cooking throughout to prevent it from becoming leathery and dry.

The cooking of game is often cited as the test of a good cook, but a cook is only as good as her ingredients, so do not be put off. Just make sure that the meat is well hung, well marinated and competently cooked.

MARINATED VENISON WITH PORT

serves 4

King Henry VII used venison fat as an ointment and there is a note in the privy purse expenses of 1505 that a certain woman was paid 3s.4d. (about 35 cents) for clarifying venison suet for the King. What medicinal use it was meant to have remains a mystery, but he obviously thought highly of it to pay such a price.

4 venison steaks

Marinade
½ teaspoon thyme   *1 glass port*
½ teaspoon chopped parsley   *salt and freshly ground black*
pinch of nutmeg   *pepper to taste*
juice and grated rind of 1 Seville
* orange or ½ sweet orange and*
* ½ lemon*

2 tablespoons oil   *1 teaspoon redcurrant jelly*

freshly chopped parsley to garnish

Flatten the venison steaks between 2 pieces of greaseproof paper with a rolling pin, remove the paper and put them in a suitable dish for marinating. Mix all the ingredients for the marinade together and pour it over the meat. Leave in a warm place for about 4 hours, basting it occasionally.

Drain the venison steaks and scrape off any of the bits of marinade which may be sticking to the surface. Wipe the steaks dry with a kitchen cloth. Heat the oil in a frying pan and gently fry the steaks on both sides until they are tender. Remove from the heat, arrange on a serving dish and keep warm. Return the pan to the heat, add the marinade and bring it to the boil, stirring it so that the meat's juices mix together. Reduce the gravy by one third of its original quantity, stir in the redcurrant jelly and simmer until it has melted. Stir thoroughly and pour over the venison. Sprinkle with freshly chopped parsley and serve immediately.

PIGEON PIQUANT

serves 2

As a general rule, tame pigeons should be cooked while they are still fresh, whereas wood pigeons should be hung for a few days.

'Slice a large onion and put it in a shallow dish, with two bayleaves, twenty juniper berries, half a tea-spoonful of peppercorns and a quarter of a pint (⅔ cup) of vinegar. Lay two pigeons in this marinade, and turn and baste them twice a day for two days. If the birds are old they will need to remain in the marinade a day or two longer. Take them up, wipe them dry, and lard the breasts evenly, then put them in a saucepan with an ounce (2 tablespoons) of butter, and turn them about over a moderate fire until they are brightly and evenly browned. Lift them out, stir a spoonful of flour in with the butter, and mix it briskly with a wooden spoon until it begins to colour, then add four ounces (½ cup) of fat bacon cut into small pieces, the liver of the birds, a cupful of stock or water, the strained juice of half a lemon with an inch or two of rind, and a little pepper, salt and grated nutmeg. Let this sauce boil then put in the pigeons, cover them closely and let them stew for half an hour. Serve the birds on a hot dish with the sauce poured round them.' – *Cassell's Dictionary of Cookery* (1890)

Note: Depending on the size and age of the pigeons, they may need up to 50 minutes cooking time to be really tender.

ROAST PARTRIDGE WITH VINE LEAVES

serves 2

Tobias Venner, writing in 1620, had some rather idiosyncratic ideas about food. Amongst other things, he thought the poor should never eat partridges as they were (according to him) calculated to promote asthma. 'Wherefore,' he continued, 'when they shall chance to meet with a covey of young partridges, they were much better to bestow them upon such, for whom they are convenient.' – from *Via Recta ad Vitam Longa* by Tobias Venner.

2 young partridges

Marinade
6-8 vine leaves (see page 136)   *1 glass white wine*

2 rashers streaky bacon   *2 tablespoons cream*

Make sure that the partridges are young and plump as older birds are not suitable for roasting, and that they have been sufficiently hung (allow 3-4 days).

Wrap the birds in the vine leaves (commercially prepared leaves should be blanched in hot water as they tend to be a little salty). Place them in a suitable dish for marinating and pour over the white wine. Leave in a cool place for 1 hour to absorb the flavours.

Tie the rashers of bacon over the breast of each bird, pour over the wine and roast them in a hot oven, 400°F, gas mark 6 for about 25-35 minutes, basting them occasionally. When they are cooked, remove them from the roasting tin and keep warm. Add the cream to the pan juices and carefully re-heat it so that it does not curdle. Serve with the gravy poured over the birds.

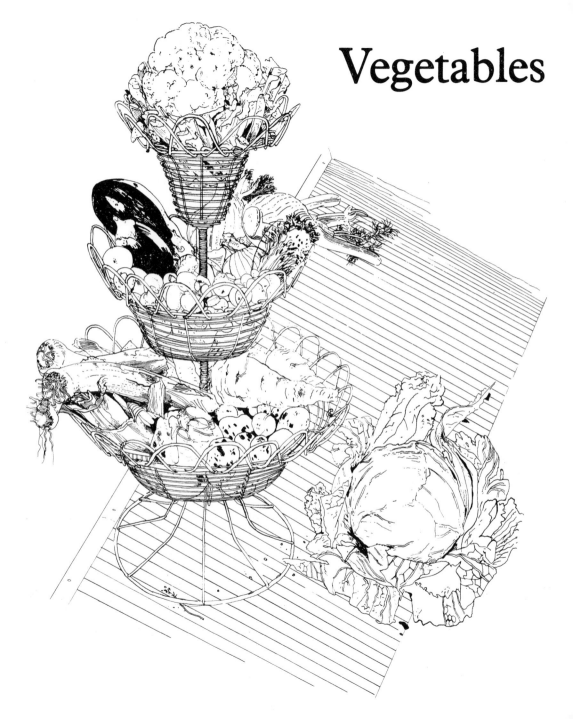

Vegetables

VEGETABLES

'The quality of vegetables depends much both on the soil in which they are grown and on the degree of care bestowed upon their culture: but if produced in ever so great perfection, their excellence will be entirely destroyed if they be badly cooked', wrote Eliza Acton: while the quality of the British vegetable may be indisputable, our reputation for cooking vegetables is non-existent.

There is no denying the fact that we generally ruin our vegetables by overcooking and reducing them to a soggy mass. Anyone who has sampled the delights of 'meat and two veg, coming up' can only agree. The great Victorian theory as set out by Miss Acton was heartily in favour of soft vegetables as 'when not sufficiently cooked (vegetables) are known to be so exceedingly unwholesome and indigestible that the custom of serving them *crisp*, which means in reality only half-boiled, should be altogether disregarded when health is considered'. The Italians thought otherwise; they happily prepared their vegetables 'al dente' and never seemed to suffer any ill effects!

They were responsible for introducing raw or 'crisp' vegetables to the French and it was from both those countries that we adopted the habit of eating vegetables as a separate course; either as hors d'oeuvre or as a salad after the main course. Most of the following recipes can be served thus or as an accompaniment to meat or fish.

I cannot overstress the importance of choosing and cooking vegetables carefully. Always use them when they are fresh and firm and discard any which may be bruised or marked. Avoid, whenever possible, frozen or tinned vegetables; they nearly always contain some preservatives or chemicals unless, of course, they are home-frozen. Wash and clean your vegetables carefully and try not to peel or skin them as most of their goodness is contained in the outer layers. Do not overcook them as apart from ruining the taste, colour and flavour, the vegetables are far more difficult to handle and are liable to break or crumble when being tossed or coated with the marinade. In the case of using uncooked vegetables, wash and dry them thoroughly before slicing or cutting them.

Most vegetables should be marinated in a cool place and some dishes (see Coriander Mushrooms, Leeks a la Grecque and White Haricot Bean Salad) will keep for up to three days in the fridge, so they can be prepared well in advance.

COURGETTES (ZUCCHINI) WITH TARRAGON

serves 4-6

A delicious low-fat dish which can be served as an hors-d'oeuvre or as an accompanying vegetable to cold chicken or veal. If possible do use fresh rather than dried tarragon as it adds a superb bitter sweet bite.

1-1½ pounds courgettes or zucchini

Marinade
2-3 sprigs fresh tarragon or   *juice of ½ lemon*
  ½ teaspoon dried tarragon   *salt and freshly ground black*
¼ pint (⅔ cup) cultured   *pepper to taste*
  buttermilk

Wash and pat the courgettes or zucchini dry with a kitchen towel. Cut into 1-inch thick slices, but do not peel them. Heat enough water to cover the bottom of a saucepan and add the courgettes or zucchini. Cover and simmer gently for about 5-10 minutes until cooked but still quite crisp. Drain and arrange in a shallow serving dish. Mix the ingredients for the marinade together and pour over. Leave to marinate in a cool place for about 2-3 hours before serving.

See colour illustration between pages 120 and 121.

4-DAY BUTTERED SPINACH

serves 6-8

Buttered spinach is an amazing treat. Brillat-Savarin recommended it when he wrote of Canon Chevrier, whose Friday spinach was always cooked on the previous Sunday and put back on the fire every day with a new dressing of butter! The spinach absorbs the butter as it reduces to a rich puree and although its preparation can continue for days, I find that after four days it is quite delicious and ready to eat.

3-4 pounds fresh spinach　　　　　*pinch of nutmeg*
　(see note)　　　　　　　　　　*1 teaspoon lemon juice*
salt and pepper to taste　　　　　*1 pound (2 cups) unsalted butter*

Wash the spinach thoroughly and discard any of the stringy stalks. Put it in a saucepan with the salt and pepper, nutmeg and lemon juice. Cook over a gentle heat until soft. It is not necessary to add any water to the pan, as the spinach will give off plenty of liquid as it cooks, but do stir it occasionally to prevent the underneath leaves from sticking to the bottom. Drain the spinach and chop it roughly. Return it to the pan and add 4 ounces (½ cup) of butter. Heat the spinach until the butter has melted and is completely absorbed. Spoon the spinach into a bowl, leave it to cool before storing it in the fridge. The following day, heat the spinach with another 4 ounces (½ cup) of butter and leave it to cool and return it to the fridge. Repeat the process on the third day, and on the fourth day, when it has been gently heated and absorbed the butter, it is ready to be eaten. As it is so rich it is best eaten with plainly grilled white fish or steak.

Note: You really must use fresh rather than tinned or frozen spinach for this recipe, otherwise the texture and taste are spoilt.

MARINATED AUBERGINES (EGG-PLANTS) I

serves 4

Aubergines, or egg-plants as they are known in America, are delicious baked and eaten either hot or cold. This recipe can be served as a starter or as a light meal in itself, in which case you should double the quantities to allow one whole aubergine (egg-plant) per person.

2 medium aubergines (egg-plants)

Marinade
1 teaspoon salt
freshly ground black pepper to
  taste
1 teaspoon basil

2-3 cloves garlic, cut into slivers
2 rashers best bacon, cut into slivers
3 tablespoons olive oil
2 tomatoes, peeled and chopped

Wash the aubergines (egg-plants) and pat them dry with a kitchen towel. Make two rows of fairly deep cuts around them with a sharp knife. Mix the salt, pepper and basil together and roll the slivers of garlic in the mixture. Stuff the cuts with a sliver of seasoned garlic alternating with a sliver of bacon. Rub the skins of the aubergines (egg-plants) with any of the remaining salt, pepper and basil mixture and arrange them in an ovenproof dish suitable for marinating. Spoon over the chopped tomatoes and pour over about 2 tablespoons of the olive oil. Leave to marinate for about 1 hour. Cover the dish and roast in a slow oven, 300°F, gas mark 2 for 1 hour. Cut the aubergines (egg-plants) in half lengthways and sprinkle with the remainder of the oil. Either serve immediately or leave to cool, basting them occasionally with the juices.

MARINATED AUBERGINES (EGG-PLANTS) II

serves 6

This spiced recipe comes from Israel where aubergines (egg-plants) grow in great profusion. Israeli cooking is a curious mixture of oriental (heavily oiled and spiced) and mid-European (bland) food, due no doubt to the influence of both the Sephardic jews who settled in the Middle East and North Africa, and the Ashkenazi jews who come from Eastern Europe.

3 medium aubergines (egg-plants) *1 teaspoon salt*

2 small green peppers, chopped   *2 cloves garlic, crushed*
2 small red peppers, chopped   *¼ pint (⅔ cup) olive oil*
2 pickled cucumbers, chopped

Marinade
¼ pint (⅔ cup) wine vinegar   *6-8 black peppercorns*
2 tablespoons water   *salt to taste*
½ teaspoon sugar   *1 dried chilli*

Wash and cut the aubergines (egg-plants) into 1-inch thick slices. Sprinkle them with salt and put them in a colander with a weight on top. Leave for about 45 minutes to allow the bitter juices to drain away. Wash and pat the aubergines (egg-plants) dry with a kitchen towel. Heat the oil and fry them, a few slices at a time, until soft. Drain on a piece of absorbent paper. Add as much oil as you find necessary as the aubergines (egg-plants) really do soak it up. When all the aubergines (egg-plants) are cooked, add the peppers, pickled cucumbers and garlic to the pan and fry until tender. Bring all the ingredients for the marinade to the boil in a saucepan, cover and simmer for about 10 minutes. Remove from the heat and leave to cool.

Meanwhile arrange the aubergines (egg-plants) in layers in a suitable flat-bottomed dish and on top of each layer spinkle a little of the cooked pepper and cucumber mixture. Pour over the unstrained vinegar mixture, making sure that it reaches the bottom layer, and leave in the fridge to marinate for about 2 days before serving.

CORIANDER MUSHROOMS

serves 6

A recipe from Elizabeth David's *Spices, Salt and Aromatics in the English Kitchen (English Cooking, Ancient & Modern 1)* Penguin Books 1970, which makes a delicious cold hors-d'oeuvre. As she points out 'the flavourings are similar to those used in champignons a la grecque, but the method is simpler, and the result even better'.

12 ounces (3 cups) firm white mushrooms

Marinade

juice of 1 lemon	*2-3 bayleaves*
5 tablespoons olive oil	*salt and freshly ground black*
2 teaspoons coriander seeds, crushed	*pepper to taste*

Clean the mushrooms and cut them into quarters. Brush them with a little of the lemon juice. Heat 4 tablespoons of the olive oil in a frying pan and add the crushed coriander seeds. Cook them for a few seconds over a gentle heat and add the mushrooms, bayleaves and salt and pepper to taste. Cook for about 1 minute, cover the pan and leave them to simmer, very gently, for a further 3-5 minutes.

Pour the mushrooms with all their juices into a dish, add the remainder of the lemon juice and olive oil. Leave to marinate in a cool place for about 3-4 hours, or up to 2 days in the refrigerator.

SPICED INDONESIAN VEGETABLES

serves 4

The Indonesians often eat their vegetables highly spiced and lightly cooked – which by our standards is really no more than a quick blanching so that they remain crisp and firmly textured. A wok, the Chinese pan with a rounded base, is the ideal cooking vessel for this method of cooking as it is wide enough to hold the food; but do not be put off if you do not have one as an ordinary large saucepan will do just as well. The essential thing is to use a pan large enough to allow the vegetables to spread out while cooking so that they are cooked evenly.

1 pound raw mixed vegetables to include: shredded cabbage; green peas; green beans; cut into 1-inch slices; carrots, cut into 1-inch slices; cauliflower, cut into flowerets; broccoli, cut into spears

Marinade
2-3 fresh chillies, crushed　　*1 small onion, grated*
¼-inch piece green ginger,　　*1 teaspoon turmeric*
　crushed　　　　　　　　*½ teaspoon salt*

½ pint (1¼ cups) good stock　　*1 teaspoon lemon grass powder or*
1 tablespoon wine vinegar　　　　*1 strip lemon peel, pared*
1 teaspoon sugar

Wash and dry the vegetables and cut them into thin pieces, using whatever selection you choose from the suggestions listed above. Pound all the ingredients for the marinade together in a pestle and mortar to make a thick paste. If you do not like your food too spicy, remove the seeds from the chillies before you crush them. Arrange the vegetables in a large flat bottomed dish and spread the paste evenly all over. Leave to marinate for about 1 hour.

Heat the stock in a wok or large saucepan (see above) and add the vinegar, sugar and lemon grass or lemon peel. Simmer the ingredients for about 2 minutes and add the vegetables. Stir them so that they separate in the stock, a pair of chopsticks is very useful for this and cook for about 2-3 minutes. Remove the vegetables from the pan with a draining spoon or strainer and arrange them in a serving dish. Bring the stock to the boil and reduce it by boiling vigorously until it starts to thicken. Pour it over the vegetables and serve immediately.

Note: A few slices of chopped ham or cooked chicken added to the stock will transform this vegetable dish into a complete and satisfying meal.

See colour illustration facing page 41.

LEEKS A LA GRECQUE

serves 6

Vegetables cooked à la grecque are simmered in a seasoned court-bouillon which is then reduced and poured over them and, as the vegetables cool, they marinate in the juices and absorb the flavours. Mushrooms, cauliflowers, carrots, onions and, of course, leeks are delicious when cooked in this method and I sometimes prepare a selection of the vegetables cooked one after the other in the court-bouillon and served arranged together. They must, however, be cooked separately to allow for the different cooking times (the vegetables should be tender but still crisp) and as a general rule I start with the more delicately flavoured vegetables, so that their taste is not drowned.

1½ pounds leeks

Court-bouillon
4-6 coriander seeds
6-8 fennel seeds
1 bayleaf
2 sprigs fresh parsley
2 sprigs fresh thyme or ½ teaspoon dried thyme

¾ pint (2 cups) water
2 tablespoons oil
juice of ½ lemon
½ teaspoon salt
10 black peppercorns

Choose small, firm leeks and trim off about ½ inch of the green tops and cut off the roots. If you prefer to cook the leeks whole, make two lengthways cuts down the top of the leeks and carefully ease back the leaves to wash them. Otherwise slice the leeks crossways and wash them under running water in a colander or sieve. Either way, make sure that all traces of grit are removed before you start cooking. Tie the coriander seeds, fennel seeds, bayleaf, parsley and thyme together in a piece of cheesecloth or muslin and place in a saucepan with the remainder of the ingredients for the court-bouillon. Heat until boiling. Turn down the heat and simmer for about 5 minutes. Add the leeks, cover the pan and simmer for about 10-15 minutes, depending on their size and simmer for about 10-15 minutes, depending on their size and thickness. Remove the leeks with a draining spoon and arrange them in a serving dish. Bring the court-bouillon to the boil and reduce it by boiling vigorously to about half its original quantity. Strain it over the leeks and leave it to cool before placing it in the fridge. Leave it to marinate for at least 6 hours before serving, although the vegetables once cooked will keep for about 4-5 days.

See colour illustration between pages 120 and 121.

CARROTS AND CARDAMOMS

serves 4-6

'Wild carrots belong to Mercury, and therefore break wind and remove stitches in the side, provoke urine and women's courses, and helpeth to break and expel the stone; . . . and though Galen commended garden carrots highly to break wind, yet experience teacheth they breed it first, and we may thank nature for expelling it, not they.' – *Culpeper's Complete Herbal* by Nicholas Culpeper

In India the cardamom, which has certain carminative properties, is cooked with carrots to aid the digestion and to avoid flatulence.

Previous page: Tandoori Chicken
This page: Coriander Mushrooms
       Coriander Olives
       Veal & Spinach Pâté
       Lemon Pickle
       Tea Leaf Eggs
       Tomato Store Sauce
       Leeks à la Grecque
       Courgettes with Tarragon
Overleaf: A selection of fresh herbs

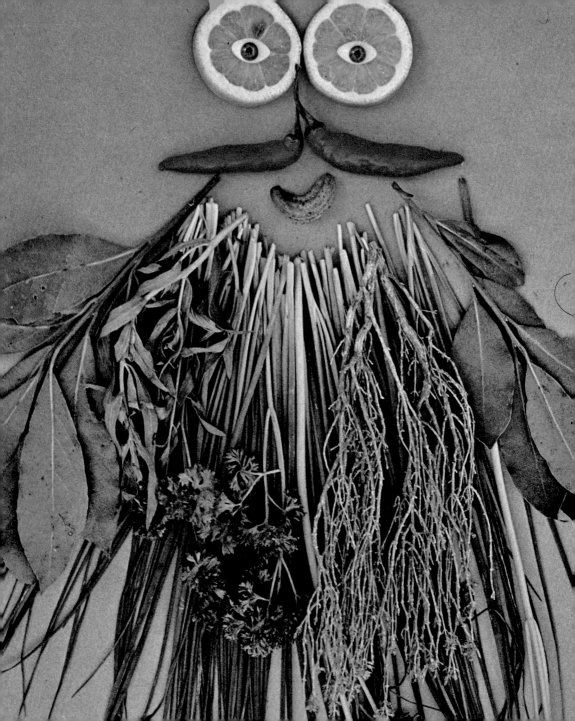

1½ pounds young carrots

Court-bouillon
1 teaspoon honey   *½ teaspoon salt*
½ pint (1¼ cups) water   *1 clove garlic, bruised*
1 tablespoon vinegar   *1 bayleaf*
2 tablespoons cider   *2 teaspoons lemon juice*
2 tablespoons olive oil   *freshly ground black pepper to taste*
2 cardamom pods, crushed

Clean and scrape the carrots (if you use young carrots, it should not be necessary to peel them) and cut them into quarters. Heat the honey in a little water until it melts and then add the remainder of the water, the vinegar, cider, olive oil, cardamoms, salt, garlic and bayleaf to the saucepan. Simmer the ingredients for about 5 minutes to extract the flavours and add the prepared carrots. Cover and cook for between 5-10 minutes, depending on how crisp you like your vegetables. Remove the carrots with a draining spoon and arrange them in a serving dish. Reduce the marinade to about half its original quantity by boiling it vigorously and remove it from the heat. Allow it to cool slightly before adding the lemon juice. Strain the marinade over the carrots and mix them together. Leave it in a cool place to marinate for a minimum of 3 hours before serving.

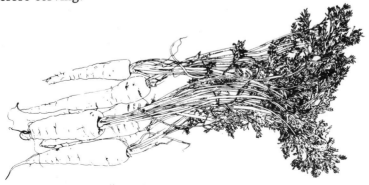

POTATO SALAD I

serves 4-6

'Let the salad-maker be a spendthrift for oil, a miser for vinegar, a statesman for salt, and a madman for mixing.' – Spanish proverb

There are so many variations for a potato salad – some better known than others – that I have only included a selection of more unusual recipes. Use firm, waxy potatoes, new potatoes are the obvious choice as they do not need peeling, and, if you buy small potatoes, it should not be necessary to slice them as they can be left whole.

1-1½ pounds new potatoes

Marinade
1 teaspoon dill weed   *salt to taste*
½ pint (1¼ cups) sour cream or
  ½ pint (1¼ cups) smetana

½ teaspoon cayenne pepper to garnish

Scrub the potatoes and cook them in lightly salted water until tender. Drain and leave them to cool slightly. Mix all the ingredients for the marinade together and pour it over the potatoes while they are still warm. Toss the potatoes so that they are thoroughly coated in the dressing and leave in a cool place for a minimum of 2 hours so that they can absorb the flavours. Serve with the cayenne pepper spinkled on top.

POTATO SALAD II

serves 4-6

1-1½ pounds new potatoes

Marinade

2 tablespoons oil
1-inch piece fresh ginger, peeled and crushed
1 teaspoon cumin seed

½ pint (1¼ cups stabilized yoghurt (see page 19)
1 teaspoon turmeric powder
pinch of chilli powder (optional)
1 teaspoon lime juice

Scrub the potatoes and cook them in lightly salted water until tender. Drain and leave them to cool slightly. Meanwhile heat the oil and fry the ginger and cumin seeds for 1 minute. Add the yoghurt, tumeric and chilli powder. Stir all the ingredients and cook for about 3-4 minutes over a low heat. Remove from the heat and add the lime juice. Pour the marinade over the potatoes while they are still warm and leave them to marinate in a cool place for about 3 hours before serving.

POTATO SALAD III

serves 4-6

'A German recipe – Cut the pound of cooked potatoes into slices the third of an inch thick, and sprinkle a little pepper and salt amongst them. Cut two or three rashers of bacon into very small pieces, and fry these over a gentle fire until they are lightly browned. Pour into the pan with them half a cupful of water (about ¼ pint) and half a cupful of vinegar (about ¼ pint), let the bacon simmer in this for a minute, and pour the sauce over the potatoes. If after soaking a little time the salad looks dry, add half a cupful of milk (about ¼ pint).' – *Cassell's Dictionary of Cookery*

WHITE HARICOT BEAN SALAD

serves 6-8

'Let onion atoms lurk within the bowl
And, scarce-suspected, animate the whole' – from *Recipe for Salad*, Sidney Smith

The secret of this salad is to add the dressing to the beans while they are still warm so they soak it up and absorb the flavours.

1 pound (2 cups) white haricot
  beans
1 clove garlic
2 slices lemon

1 bayleaf
½ teaspoon salt
water

Marinade
2 onions, finely chopped
1 clove garlic, crushed
1 teaspoon prepared mustard
½ pint (1¼ cups) buttermilk
2 tablespoons oil

1 tablespoon vinegar
2 ounces (¼ cup) salami, chopped
  (optional)
salt and freshly ground black
  pepper to taste

freshly chopped parsley to garnish

Wash the beans and leave them to soak overnight in water to allow them to swell up. Drain and put them in a saucepan with the garlic, lemon slices, bayleaf and salt and add sufficient water to the depth of 2 inches above the beans. Bring the water to the boil, cover the saucepan and cook for about 1½ hours or until the beans are tender but not too soft. Drain the beans, remove the garlic and lemon slices and leave them to cool slightly.

To make the marinade, mix all the ingredients together and while the beans are still warm, pour it over them. Stir carefully so as not to crush the beans but make sure that the salad is thoroughly tossed. Leave for about 3-4 hours, longer if possible, before serving. Decorate the top with plenty of freshly chopped parsley.

ONION SALAD

serves 4

Raw onions can taste quite harsh and can be quite difficult to digest because of their high content of volatile oil. One way to remedy this is to blanch them in boiling water before use; but a more satisfactory method is to marinate them in a herb vinegar, which has the advantage of flavouring them at the same time.

2 large onions

Marinade
½ teaspoon salt   *3 tablespoons mint vinegar (see page 131) or 3 tablespoons wine vinegar and 1 teaspoon chopped mint*

Peel and cut the onions into thin slices and arrange them in a suitable dish for marinating. Sprinkle over the salt and add the flavoured vinegar or the vinegar and the mint. If you think that the flavour of your vinegar is not strong enough, you can always add an extra pinch of mint. Toss the salad so that the onions are coated with vinegar and leave it in a cool place for about 2 hours, turning it occasionally, to marinate. Serve it as an hors-d'oeuvre or as a side salad with the main course.

Note: The marinated onions also make a delicious flavouring for a savoury yoghurt. Drain the onions first to remove most of the vinegar and add 1 tablespoon of onions for every 2 tablespoons of yoghurt used.

RAITA – CUCUMBER SALAD

serves 4-6

Raita is a refreshing salad which is often served with Tandoori Chicken (see page 42) to provide a cooling contrast in tastes. An interesting departure from the better known yoghurt, cucumber and mint raita, this recipe was kindly given to me by the Shezan, a restaurant in London famous for its Indian food. My American readers will be pleased to know that they have recently opened a branch in New York.

½ cucumber	½ teaspoon salt

Marinade
1 pint (1¼ cups) fresh yoghurt	freshly ground black pepper
2 ounces (6 tablespoons) raisins	½ teaspoon ground cumin

Peel and slice the cucumber and sprinkle it with salt. Press it lightly between two plates for about 15 minutes and drain it to remove the liquid. Mix the cucumber with the yoghurt and raisins in a serving bowl and add the black pepper to taste. Sprinkle the top with the cumin and place it in the fridge. Leave for about 3 hours before serving.

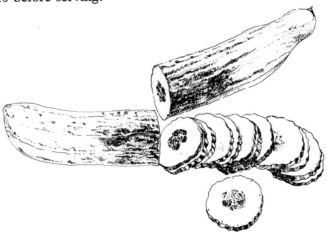

BASIL AND TOMATO SALAD

serves 4-6

Basil and tomatoes are one of the most delightful combinations of taste and in order to derive full benefit of the flavours, the salad should be prepared in advance and left to marinate. It is best to use fresh basil (I try to keep a pot growing throughout the year in my kitchen as it is an annual which withers at the first hint of frost), but failing that, dried basil does retain its flavour well and can always be used instead.

4-6 firm, sweet tomatoes (see note)

Marinade
1 teaspoon chopped basil leaves   *1 tablespoon olive oil*
* or ½ teaspoon dried basil*   *1 teaspoon lemon juice*
salt and freshly ground black
* pepper to taste*

4-6 black olives, stoned, to garnish

Wash and pat dry the tomatoes. With a sharp knife cut them into fairly thin slices and arrange them in a shallow dish. Sprinkle the basil on top and add salt and pepper to taste. Mix the olive oil with the lemon juice and pour over the tomatoes. Leave to marinate in the fridge for about 1 hour. Serve chilled, decorated with the olives.

Note: Try to use either Italian or Moroccan tomatoes as they are both firm and very sweet.

Pickles & Preserves

PICKLES & PRESERVES

'Nothing shows more' wrote Mrs. Beeton, 'the difference between a tidy, thrifty housewife and a lady to whom these desirable epithets may not honestly be applied, than the appearance of their respective store closets.' Since then the practice of keeping a cupboard stocked with pickles, preserves and other such delights has become neglected in favour of bought preparations. We have become lazy and prepared to sacrifice our ancestors' high standards of quality and flavour to the pressures of modern living and convenience foods.

Admittedly, certain bought pickles are delicious, but with a very small amount of extra effort, we can easily make our own. They are cheaper, fun to make and make delightful presents. The satisfaction of opening a cupboard filled with jars crammed with fresh, unadulterated ingredients is immeasurable and certainly worth the effort.

For years I have been collecting old recipes for pickles and sauces (early cookery books are irresistible but sadly are becoming astonomically expensive to buy) and I love trying them out. The secret is to use fresh ingredients when they are in season – that way you are sure of their quality and it works out a lot cheaper. Always wash and dry vegetables thoroughly before using them and make sure that they are in prime condition.

The principle of pickling is essentially one of marinating. Ingredients, either raw or cooked, are soaked in a flavoured liquid (usually oil or vinegar) and are preserved by the reaction of this liquid on the ingredients. If stored in airtight glass or earthenware – but never plastic – containers, they will keep for months, provided of course you do not eat them first!

Some of the following recipes (see Coriander Olives, Store Tomato Sauce, Pickled Nasturtium Seeds) can themselves be used as ingredients in a marinade; others make a tasty addition to a salad or a dish of fish or cold meats.

FLAVOURED VINEGARS

The Greeks and Romans used vinegar in their cookery and as a medicine. Apparently Roman soldiers always carried a ration of vinegar which they would mix with water to make a refreshing drink that quenched their thirst during battle.

Nowadays we use vinegar mainly in salad dressings, sauces, marinades and pickles. Although vinegar can be made from wine, or malt, or sugar and water, and also from a vinegar plant or 'mother', most of us prefer to buy vinegar as it is a lot less trouble.

Flavoured vinegars are made from herbs or spices or a mixture of the two with either commercially prepared or home-made vinegar. They are easy to make and really do add subtle aroma to an ordinary vingar. Start with a good quality vinegar (wine vinegar is preferable) and follow the directions according to the recipes below. I keep a selection in my store cupboard and use them as and when required. One word of advice, do not forget to label each bottle clearly – otherwise they can get easily confused and you will not know which flavour you end up using!

CHILLI VINEGAR

'Cut 100 small, fresh red chillies into halves and infuse them for a fortnight in a quart (5 cups) of best pickling vinegar. Strain the liquid and put it into small bottles. It is convenient to have this vinegar at hand to flavour sauces and to serve with fish. The vinegar will keep a long time if closely corked'.

TARRAGON VINEGAR

'Gather the tarragon on a dry day, just before the plant begins to bloom. This will be late in July, or in the early part of August. Pick the leaves from the stalks, and with them fill wide-mouthed glass bottles up to the neck, and in doing so bruise the leaves slightly that their flavour may more easily escape. Cover with best vinegar, tie bladder over the mouths of the bottles, and then let the leaves infuse six weeks or two months. Pour off the liquid, strain through muslin till it is quite clear, pour it into small bottles and cork down securely. Store in a dry place'.

Note: The Victorians used bladder to seal their jars and to make them airtight.

GARLIC VINEGAR

'Take three ounces of the cloves of garlic (6 large cloves), remove the skin and bruise them slightly in a mortar. Put them into an earthen jar, with a teaspoonful of salt, half a dozen cloves, and half an ounce of whole ginger. Pour over them a quart (5 cups) of best vinegar, cover closely, and in ten days or a fortnight strain off for use. Two or three drops will prove a valuable addition to sauces and salads. The flavour may be increased or diminished by leaving the garlic a longer or shorter time in the vinegar, or by altering the proportion of garlic. Before straining off for use taste two or three drops, and see if the flavour is such as will be liked'.

GREEN MINT VINEGAR

'Take some freshly-gathered mint, pick off the leaves, chop them slightly, and fill wide-necked bottles with them. Pour over some good French vinegar, and let them infuse for two months or more. Strain through muslin into small bottles, cork securely, and put aside for use.
Note: French vinegar is a good wine vinegar.

SEASONED VINEGAR FOR SALADS

'Take of shallots three ounces (¾ cup), of tarragon, savory, and chives, three ounces (2 cups) each, and balm and mint one ounce (¾ cup) each; dry these ingredients very carefully, and bruise them. Put them in a wide-mouthed bottle, pour upon them a gallon (20 cups) of vinegar, and cork the bottle securely. Put it in a warm place, leave it for two or three weeks till the vinegar is strongly flavoured, pour off the liquor, and press the herbs very dry with a spoon. Let the vinegar stand to settle for a few hours, filter it, and put it into small bottles. Cork closely and store for use'.

Recipes from *Cassell's Dictionary of Cookery* (1890)

PICKLED NASTURTIUM SEEDS (to taste like capers)

During the last War, the British Government launched a campaign called 'Dig for Victory'. Its object was to encourage everyone to grow as much of their own food as possible. The public were also urged to try various wild plants which were nutritious and perfectly safe to eat. The nasturtium was one of the most versatile of these – its leaves made a delicious filling for sandwiches, the flowers were added to soups and salads, and its seeds were ground for a substitute pepper or pickled to make an excellent imitation caper.

'The seeds must be green and young, and gathered in fine weather. After wiping them, put them in a weak brine for two days and nights; then drain them and let them lie in fresh water for twelve hours. Then drain them again and pack them into bottles, so that they are not quite full, and add a little grated horse-radish. Now boil some white wine vinegar with a little salt, a dozen peppercorns and half a tea-spoonful of mixed spices (whole) to each pint (2½ cups) of vinegar. While the vinegar is hot, strain it into the bottles, and cover these down when the contents are cold.'

– *Cooking in War Time* by Ambrose Heath (Nicholson & Watson, 1939)

MARINATED ARTICHOKE HEARTS

One of the simplest tips that I learnt from a great Italian cook is to keep a jar of seasoned artichoke hearts ever ready in the kitchen, to brighten up a plain green salad. I find that if I make a large jarful at one time, it lasts for weeks.

1 large tin artichoke hearts

Marinade
4 slices of lemon   *2-3 bayleaves*
pinch of salt   *1 clove*
½ teaspoon whole peppercorns   *olive oil*

Drain the artichoke hearts and discard the brine. Pack them into a screw-top or rubber-sealed, glass storage jar. Add the slices of lemon, salt, peppercorns, bayleaves and clove. Pour over enough good olive oil to cover them. It is important that they are completely covered with oil, otherwise they tend to go mouldy and sour. Seal the jar and store it in the fridge, using the artichoke hearts as required to flavour or decorate salads.

When the jar is nearly empty, repeat the process, always making sure that there is plenty of olive oil.

CORIANDER OLIVES

Another interesting idea which comes from Greece is to marinate plain green olives. Make sure you buy firm, plump olives which have not already been stuffed or flavoured.

8 ounces (1¼ cups) green olives

Marinade
1 teaspoon coriander seeds,
 crushed
2 cloves of garlic, peeled and
 lightly bruised

2 slices of lemon
1 tablespoon olive oil

With a sharp knife make a little cut in each olive. You can, if you are very particular, remove the stones but it is a rather time-consuming task and not really necessary. Put the olives in a screw-top or rubber-sealed, glass storage jar and add the coriander seeds, garlic, lemon slices and oil. Seal the jar and shake it vigorously so that all the ingredients are thoroughly mixed together. Leave in a cool place for 5-7 days before trying them.

They are delicious served on their own or with slices of feta – the Greek goat's cheese – as a cocktail snack, or as a stuffing for a baked fish.

See colour illustration between pages 120 and 121.

TOMATO STORE SAUCE

This really is a delicious sauce which can be used instead of ketchup or a concentrated tomato purée – but I must admit that I have been unable to make it keep for longer than two weeks, unless stored in the fridge.

'Take a dozen ripe tomatoes, put them in an earthen jar, and set them in a cool oven until they are quite soft. Take off the skins and stalks, mix with the tomatoes the liquor that flowed from them when baked, and add 2 teaspoons of salt, 2 teaspoons of powdered ginger, a pinch of cayenne, and two table-spoonfuls of vinegar. Mix the ingredients thoroughly, put the sauce into dry wide-mouthed bottles and store in a cool dry place. Examine and taste it at the end of a week or a fortnight, and if it does not seem that it would keep, boil it again with a little more cayenne and ginger. This sauce will keep for a long time. It will not be properly flavoured till ten days or a forthnight after it is made, though it may be used at once. Some cooks add a head of garlic to the other ingredients, but this not generally liked'. – *Cassell's Dictionary of Cookery, 1890.*

See colour illustration between pages 120 and 121.

LEMON PICKLE

The difference between an Indian pickle and chutney lies in their preparation. Pickles are made from raw ingredients which are then marinated in oil, whereas chutneys are generally cooked first and then sealed with vinegar. Both take at least one week to mature, and in India the process is quickened by exposing the jars to the sun for the first few days.

12 lemons
4 ounces (⅓ cup) salt
3 cloves garlic, bruised
4 red chillies, sliced (see note)
6-8 black peppercorns

2 ounces (6 tablespoons) mustard
  seed
½ ounce (1½ tablespoons)
  fenugreek seeds
1 pint (2½ cups) oil

Wash the lemons and dry thoroughly. Cut into quarters and rub them with the salt. Put the lemons with the garlic, chillies and peppercorns into an airtight jar. Meanwhile roast the mustard and fenugreek seeds until crisp (this can either be done under a hot grill, in a dry frying pan or in a warm oven) and then grind them with a mortar and pestle to a smooth paste. Add them to the jar and pour in the oil. Seal, the jar, give it a thorough shake and store in a warm dry place. Shake the jar every three days and leave it for about 10 days, although the longer it is left the better it becomes. Serve with poached fish.

Note: For a milder pickle, remove the seeds from the chillies.

See colour illustration between pages 120 and 121.

TURNIP AND CABBAGE PICKLE

Turnips are often used as the base for pickles. Their crisp texture really gives you something to bite on. It is best made during late winter, when both cabbages and turnips are in season.

1 white cabbage, weighing 2-3 pounds
2 turnips, peeled and sliced
3 fresh chillies, sliced

4-6 juniper berries, crushed
3 tablespoons salt
2-3 pints (5-7½ cups) water
3 tablespoons gin

Wash the cabbage and shred the leaves. Leave it in a colander for 24 hours to dry, turning it occasionally to air it. Arrange the cabbage in layers with the turnips, chillies and juniper berries in a large screw-top or rubber-sealed, glass jar, packing it down quite tightly. In a saucepan dissolve the salt in the water over a low heat and leave it to cool before adding the gin. Pour the mixture over the cabbage, seal it and leave it in a warm airy place for 1 week before trying it. Once it has been opened, store it in the fridge and use as required with cold meats.

PRESERVED VINE LEAVES

In our garden we had a large vine covering a south-facing wall. Strong and sturdy it never, in spite of endless coaxing, produced one single bunch of grapes. Its leaves were enormous, great green fans with pointed ends, and as a child I would make them into hats to protect my tortoise from the glaring sun.

It was not until much later that I learn the joys of eating those leaves and it became a family tradition to have an annual preserving session when we would prepare the leaves. If you do not have your own vine (I am always amazed to see how many English gardens or greenhouses do sport them) do try and beg, borrow or steal a bunch of leaves from a friend or neighbour.

1 large bunch vine leaves   *salt to taste*
olive oil to cover

Pick at least 20 unblemished leaves and wash them carefully under a running cold tap so as not to bruise them. Plunge the leaves into lightly salted boiling water and blanch them for 1 minute. Drain and spread out the leaves to allow them to dry. In a wide necked screw-top or rubber-sealed, glass storage jar, lay the leaves flat, one on top of the other, packing them down quite tightly. Add a pinch of salt and enough olive oil to completely cover the leaves. Seal the jar and leave for at least 3-4 weeks before using them. They are delicious chopped and mixed with a salad, stuffed and rolled with a little spiced rice (dolmades) or wrapped round partridges to delicately flavour them (see recipe for Wrapped Partridges, page 110).

TEA LEAF EGGS

Tea leaf eggs are the Chinese equivalent of pickled eggs. The shells are finely cracked so the eggs absorb the flavour and colour of the spiced tea and emerge finely marked like a smooth piece of delicately veined marble.

6 eggs

Marinade
¾ pint (2 cups) water　　　　　*1 dessertspoon soy sauce*
1 whole star anise　　　　　　*½ teaspoon salt*
2 tea bags

Hard boil the eggs for 10 minutes. When they are cooked, remove them from the heat and place them in the saucepan under a running cold tap until they are cool enough to handle. Take the eggs in your hand and gently tap the shells with a spoon until they are slightly cracked. Do not remove the shells.

Heat the water in a saucepan with the tea bags, star anise, soy sauce and salt and simmer for 10 minutes. Add the eggs, cover the pan, insert a heat-diffusing mat between the heat source and pan, and simmer over a very low heat for about 1 hour, adding more water as required to ensure that the eggs are submerged in water. Remove the pan from the heat and leave the eggs to stand in the liquid in a cool place for a maximum of 8 hours. The longer you leave the eggs, the stronger they taste, but after 8 hours the flavour becomes a little too strong. Peel the eggs and serve as an hors-d'oeuvre or as a garnish to a salad.

See colour illustration between pages 120 and 121.

MRS. BEETON'S PICKLED EGGS

These should be made at about Easter when eggs are plentiful and cheap. A store of pickled eggs are most useful and add an ornamental touch to many first and second courses.

16 eggs
1 quart (5 cups) vinegar
½ ounce (2 tablespoons) black
  pepper

½ ounce (2 tablespoons) Jamaica
  (cayenne) pepper
1 ounce (2 tablespoons) ginger

'Boil the eggs for 12 minutes, then dip them into cold water, and take off the shells. Put the vinegar, with the black pepper, cayenne pepper and ginger, into a stewpan, and let it simmer for 10 minutes. Now place the eggs in a jar, pour over them the vinegar mixture, boiling hot, and, when cold, tie them down with a bladder to exclude the air. This pickle will be ready for use in a month.'

Fruit

FRUIT

It was not until the seventeenth century that the use of sugar was fully appreciated. It was then discovered that it could be used as a flavouring and as an important ingredient in preserving fruit and in making jams. Suddenly its popularity increased and demand far out-stripped supply; it became such a sought after commodity that France was even prepared to hand over the whole of the Canadian provinces for the return of Guadelope, a sugar-producing state.

Nowadays, we use a vast amount of sugar, in spite of various warnings issued by health authorities and dieticians about the dangers of the 'white menace', but it is fair to say that it is only refined sugar which is supposedly not good for us, and consequently there has been a move towards the more natural sweeteners such as honey, molasses and unrefined brown sugar. So, in all the following recipes do feel free to substitute whatever sweetener you choose.

Sugar is a necessary ingredient in the preparation of fruit. A recipe for candied fruit, which I found in an old country-wives' recipe book, states firmly that a syrup must be made 'with one pound of good sugar and half a tea-cup of water.' The preserved or dried fruit is then stirred in the boiling sugar until it crystallises. Then it is dried in an oven or before an open fire taking care that it is not allowed to discolour or turn brown. Bottled fruits are also simply made. The prepared fruit is packed in a jar with its equal weight in sugar. It is topped up every day with wine or brandy or whatever liqueur is chosen until all the sugar is dissolved. The jar is then sealed and the fruit is left to mature for about six months before it is opened. A quicker method to bottle fruit is to boil a syrup before adding it to the fruit and I have included a selection of recipes using this method.

Unfortunately I could not include all the different ways of marinating fruit (or macerating as it is correctly known), but certain favourites like soaking a fruit salad in a mixture of orange and lemon juice with ground almonds are sufficiently well known to be left out. Always choose fresh, unmarked fruit for marinating and, if it is to remain unpeeled, make sure that it is washed and thoroughly dried before it is prepared. Try to avoid over handling soft fruits as they bruise easily and will loose their juice. The appearance of fruit is also important and if it is carefully arranged in little dishes or in long stemmed cocktail glasses with a wafer or a sweet biscuit as an accompaniment, it cannot fail to make a delicious finish to a satisfying meal.

'CHAMPAGNE' STRAWBERRIES

serves 4-6

Believe it or not, substituting ginger ale for champagne really works. Use a sparkling dry ginger ale (American dry by Schweppes is best) and serve the strawberries really chilled. It is, as a friend commented, 'the ultimate swizz', but if it works, why worry?

1 pound (3 cups) fresh strawberries   *½ pint (1¼ cups) ginger ale*

Prepare the strawberries as directed in the previous recipe and arrange them in a serving dish. Pour over the ginger ale and carefully turn the strawberries to coat them in the liquid. Leave them to marinate in the fridge for a minimum of 2 hours, but if you like them really chilled, put them in the freezer compartment for the last 15 minutes. Serve with lashings of whipped cream.

Note: Strawberries can also be marinated in red or white wine, lemon juice melted with a touch of honey or even, as is sometimes found in Northern Italy, a few drips of wine vinegar mixed with syrup.

CARAMEL ORANGES

serves 6

'Knowest thou the Land where groves of citron flower,
The golden Orange darkling leaves embower –
Knowest thou the land? Oh there! Oh there!
I long with thee, my loved one, to repair.' – Goethe

The romance of the sweetly-scented orange grove with the white delicately shaped flowers symbolizing chastity and the golden sun fruit has been written about for centuries. Oranges have been cultivated almost since the beginning of civilization and are best suited to the warm sunny climate of the Mediterranean and California.

6 juicy oranges

Marinade
8 ounces (1 cup) sugar　　　　*¼ pint (⅔ cup) warm water*
¼ pint (⅔ cup) cold water

Wash and dry the oranges. With a potato peeler, pare the peel carefully from 1 orange so as not to remove the pith and cut the peel into thin match-stick strips. Cook the strips in boiling water for 1 minute, drain, refresh in cold water and set aside. To prepare the oranges, peel and pare them to remove the pith and cut them into thin slices, saving the juice. Arrange the oranges in a serving dish, strain the orange juice and pour it over and sprinkle the top with the orange rind.

Meanwhile, dissolve the sugar in a saucepan with the cold water over a low heat. When it has completely dissolved, allow it to boil for a few minutes until it turns a rich brown. Remove the saucepan from the heat and place the bottom in cold water to prevent any further cooking. Then add the warm water, return the pan to the heat and cook until the syrup is smooth and thick. Allow it to cool before pouring it over the oranges. Marinate in a cool place for 2-3 hours before serving.

SATSUMAS IN ROSE-WATER

serves 4-6

Satsumas are one of the traditional Christmas fruits, their arrival in the shops heralds the beginning of the annual festivities. It is important to use the early young, fresh fruit as their skins are softer and quite thin and so the flavour can penetrate more easily.

4-6 young satsumas

Marinade
8 ounces (1 cup) sugar   *2 teaspoons rose-water*
½ pint (1¼ cups) water

1 ounce (¼ cup) flaked almonds to garnish

Wash and dry the satsumas. Prick each satsuma with a pointed orange stick about 4-5 times all over the skin. Dissolve the sugar in the water over a low heat, and when it is completely melted, add the unpeeled satsumas. Simmer over a gentle heat for about 10-15 minutes and then remove from the heat. Put the satsumas in a serving dish and add the rose-water to the syrup. Pour the mixture over the fruit and leave them to marinate in a cool place for about 2-3 hours. Serve the satsumas whole, garnished with the almonds in the syrup. The skins, provided the satsumas are quite fresh, can also be eaten and they are surprisingly tasty, infused with the rose-water.

PEACHES IN CHAMPAGNE

serves 6

Bellini, the ultimate luxury cocktail is the speciality of Harry's Bar in Venice. I first sipped this divine drink at the precocious age of eleven, when it went straight to my head and heart! Sliced peaches in champagne are also very good with the added benefit of being able to eat and drink at the same time! For the budget conscious, I suggest the cheaper Asti Spumante or methode champenoise sparkling white wines or, failing that, you can always resort to ginger ale (see recipe for 'Champagne' Strawberries).

6 large ripe peaches

Marinade
juice of 1 orange
1 teaspoon lemon juice

1 pint (2½ cups) champagne or
sparkling white wine or ginger ale

Skin the peaches and slice them finely removing the stones. Prick the slices with a fork and arrange them in individual serving dishes. Mix any peach juice which may have collected while they were being prepared with the orange and lemon juice, and strain and pour it over the peaches. Add the champagne and carefully turn the slices so that they are coated in the juices. Leave to marinate in the fridge for 2-3 hours. Serve chilled straight from the fridge.

PINEAPPLE SHELLS

serves 4-6

As I find pineapple rather difficult to peel without losing too much of its juice, I generally serve it scooped out and arranged in its shell. It may be rather lazy, but it certainly does look most appealing.

1 medium, ripe pineapple

Marinade
6 ounces (¾ cup) sugar   *½ teaspoon ground ginger*
¾ pint (2 cups) water   *½ teaspoon ground cinnamon*
peel of 1 lemon   *2 tablespoons rum*

Cut the pineapple in half lengthways and with a serrated knife, loosen the inner core and flesh, taking care not to cut the skin. Remove the core and scoop out the flesh and cut it into thin slices. Return the pineapple to one of the cleaned halves and arrange it in layers, piling it evenly so that it does not overbalance. To prepare the marinade, dissolve the sugar in the water over a low heat with the lemon peel, ground ginger and cinnamon. Once the sugar has melted, slowly bring it to the boil until it has reduced to about half its original quantity. Strain the syrup and leave it to cool. Add the rum and pour the mixture over the pineapple. Leave it in a cool place to marinate for about 2-3 hours before serving.

FROSTED GRAPES

Although this recipe is not strictly speaking a marinade, grapes prepared like this look so attractive and taste quite delicious, that I thought I would include it. Any fruit can be frosted – small apples, firm Victoria plums, luscious apricots, dark red sweet cherries, mouth-sized greengages, sweet gooseberries. I often prepare a bowl full of frosted fruit which makes an attractive centre-piece for a special dinner party.

1 bunch black or green grapes, weighing 1-2 pounds

1 egg white, beaten stiff   *8 ounces (1 cup) caster sugar or
                                      icing sugar*

Wipe the grapes with a damp cloth and leave them to dry in a colander for about 2 hours. Hold the bunch of grapes by its stalk and carefully dip it into the stiff egg white. Turn the grapes carefully until they are coated in egg white. Spread the sugar on to a flat surface (a pastry board with a sheet of greaseproof paper will do) and, pressing very lightly, roll the grapes in the sugar until it adheres to the grapes in a thin layer. Put the grapes on a flat plate and place them in a fridge for about 5-6 hours, or until the sugar hardens. This process can be quickened by putting the grapes in the freezer compartment for a short time. Serve the grapes chilled.

PEARS IN VODKA

This recipe, which comes from France, suggests using eau de vie, but as I find it difficult to buy in England and incredibly expensive, I substitute vodka instead with amazingly good results. As in the preceding recipe, the pears must be kept for at least 6 weeks in the liquid (although the longer it keeps, the stronger the flavour) then the pears can be eaten and the vodka can be strained and drunk as a liqueur.

2 pounds hard pears

8 ounces (1 cup) sugar	*pinch of aniseed*
½ pint (1¼ cups) water	*vodka to cover*

Wash the pears and cut them into quarters. Pack them in a wide-necked glass jar or bottle. Meanwhile, melt the sugar in the water to make a clear syrup and remove from the heat. Stir in the aniseed and leave it to cool. Once the liquid has cooled pour it over the pears and add the vodka until the fruit is covered in liquid. The proportions can vary depending on the size of your container, but in order to get the full benefit of the flavours, you should use at least 1 pint (2½ cups) of vodka to ½ pint (1¼ cups) of syrup. Seal the bottle and store it in a cool place for a minimum of 6 weeks before trying it.

STRAWBERRIES IN ORANGE JUICE

serves 4-6

'It was Monsieur le Comte de la Place who discovered a very special way of treating strawberries, by moistening them with the juice of a sweet orange (the apple of Hesperides). Another savant has further improved on this recipe by adding the outer rind of the orange which he rubs off with a lump of sugar; and he claims to have proved, through a fragment of a manuscript saved from the torches which destroyed the library of Alexandria, that this was the way strawberries were seasoned at the banquets on Mount Ida.' – from *Odds and Ends* by Brillat-Savarin

1 pound (3 cups) fresh strawberries

Marinade
2 juicy oranges   *2 tablespoons water*
2 sugar lumps

Choose firm, ripe strawberries. Wipe them with a damp cloth – strawberries should never be washed or soaked in water – and hull and cut them in half. Arrange them in a serving dish. Wash and dry the oranges and rub the sugar lumps firmly over the oranges so that they soak up the zest. Melt the sugar in the water over a gentle heat until it dissolves to form a thick syrup and leave it to cool. Meanwhile, squeeze the oranges and then add the strained juice to the cooled liquid. Pour the mixture over the prepared strawberries and turn them carefully so that they are coated in the juice. Leave them to marinate for about 1 hour in a cool place.

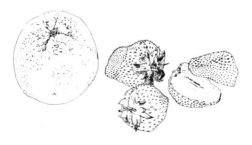

PRUNES IN BRANDY

Once the prunes have been prepared and sealed in their jar, they really ought to be left for at least 6 weeks before eating. The prunes swell up with the syrup and it takes at least that length of time for the flavours to mature. The prunes are quite delicious and can be served on their own or with whipped cream and I find that they are a superb emergency pudding. Incidentally, if the level of the jar looks a little low after constant raiding, you can always top it up with a few more prunes and a little syrup to keep a jar going continuously.

1 pound (2⅔ cups) dried prunes

Marinade
pared rind of 1 orange   *¾ pint (2 cups) water*
1 cinnamon stick, crushed   *brandy to cover*
1 tablespoon honey

Wash the prunes in cold water and dry them thoroughly. Pack them loosely in a wide-necked glass jar with the orange rind and cinnamon stick. Meanwhile, melt the honey in the water until it is completely dissolved and leave it to cool. When it is cooled pour it over the prunes and top up with brandy so that they are completely submerged in liquid. Seal the jar and give it a good shake. Leave it in a cool place for about six weeks before trying them.

Note: As the prunes swell, you may find that you will need to add extra brandy to the jar to ensure that they remain covered in syrup.

SUGARED FRUIT

serves 4-6

Goela Djawa, Javanese brown sugar, is richly flavoured with a slight nutty taste. It is superb with fruit as it adds a richness which is lacking in the more conventional and refined sugars. I buy it from Robert Jackson Ltd, 170 Piccadilly, London W1, but failing that you can use unrefined barbados sugar, which can easily be bought from most health-food shops.

1 pound ripe plums

Marinade
4 ounces (½ cup) goela djawa   *2 tablespoons white rum*
or barbados sugar

Wash and dry the plums, cut them in half and remove the stones. Arrange the plums in a serving dish and sprinkle them with the sugar, (goela djawa is sometimes in the form of a hard, solid 'cake', so it may need to be melted first in a little water before use). Pour over the rum and turn the fruit. Leave it for a minimum of 8 hours in the fridge so that the fruit can absorb the syrup. Serve chilled, straight from the fridge.

Note: Instead of rum you may like to try this recipe with white wine or orange juice.

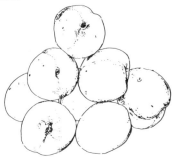

Liqueurs & Wines

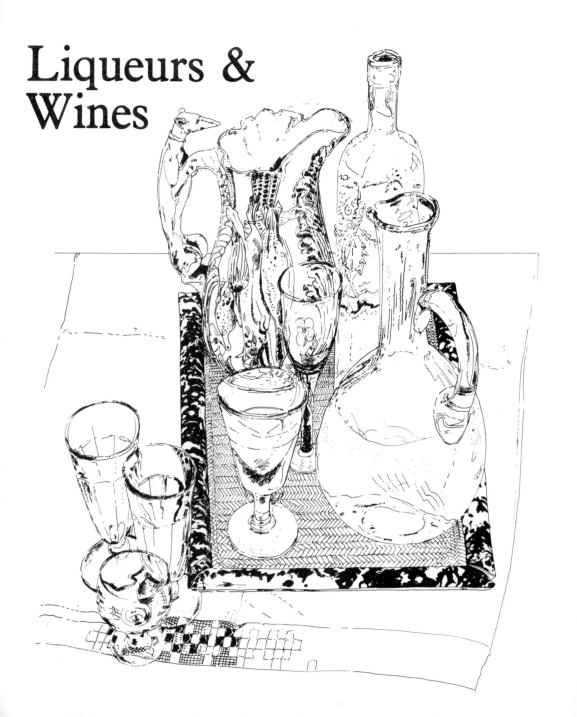

LIQUEURS & WINES

'Fill ev'ry glass, for wine inspires us,
And fires us
With courage, love and joy.
Women and wine should life employ.
Is there aught else on earth desirous?'
– *The Beggar's Opera*, John Gay

The tradition of home-made liqueurs, ratafias or fruit drinks is primarily a French one. They use marc, eau de vie and brandy, which are infused with fruit or herbs until a delicate drink results. These 'wines' are simple to make as they are not fermented and distilled, although it is apparently illegal to sell them under our licensing laws!

Although spirits are no longer as cheap as they were at one time, when brandy was considered a rough labourer's drink, these liqueurs are well worth the initial expenditure. They are quite uniquely flavoured, the fruit can be eaten separately and impart a taste which cannot be bought from any shop.

APRICOT AND CINNAMON LIQUEUR

'Peel and cut into pieces as many ripe apricots as you may require, and boil them in white wine (about a pint (2½ cups) to four dozen) with a stick of cinnamon; strain and mix it with an equal quantity of brandy; put the whole in a jar, with the kernels bruised, add a quarter of a pound (½ cup) of sugar to each pint (2½ cups). Let it infuse for three weeks, then filter and bottle it'.

– *Cook's Dictionary* by Richard Dolby, 1830

ANGELICA LIQUEUR

Angelica, according to ancient folk-lore, is the herbs of angels. It is said to bloom on the day of Michael the Archangel, to have powers of protection against evil spirits and witchcraft, and to have been revealed by an angel in a dream as the cure to a plague which was the scourge of the countryside.

Its use as a sweetener dates from a time when saccharin matter was extremely rare and it has long been used to flavour drinks. Mr. Roberts, the famous jam maker from Chelsea, made a delicious liqueur or digestive to be drunk after a meal. His recipe is as follows:

'1 ounce (3 tablespoons) of the freshly gathered stem of angelica is chopped up and steeped in 2 pints (5 cups) of good brandy during 5 days. 1 ounce (¼ cup) of skinned bitter almonds reduced to a pulp being added. The liquid is then strained through fine muslin and is sweetened with 1 pint (2½ cups) of liquid sugar.'

Note: Rhubarb and gooseberries are excellent when stewed in this liqueur instead of water.

CHERRY VODKA

The best cherry to use is the Napoleon or Kent Bigarreau, a pretty, pale yellow dessert cherry covered with a pink flush as it is pleasantly sweet with a firm crisp fruit.

1 pound cherries   *1½ pints (3¾ cups) vodka*

Wash and dry the cherries and leave them to stand overnight in a colander. Cut their stalks down to about 2-3 inches long and prick each cherry about 4-5 times with a needle or a pointed cocktail stick. Put the cherries in an airtight glass jar or bottle and pour over the vodka, so that the cherries are well and truly submerged in it. Seal the jar and leave it for at least 2 months, although it will keep for years. To serve, pour a little in a glass with a cherry which will be quite delicious to eat.

FRUIT SALAD BRANDY

Once you have started a bottle of fruit brandy, it can carry on for ever – provided, of course, that you do not drink it all up in one go! You just add extra fruit peel, (orange, lemon, apple, pear, apricot, even grape skins) from whatever fruit you may have been eating and top it up occasionally with brandy and syrup as and when it is needed. The flavour of the fruit and brandy is superb and the longer it lasts, the more potent it becomes.

To start a fruit salad brandy, use the following.

4 juicy oranges
8 ounces (1 cup) sugar
½ pint (1¼ cups) water

1 cinnamon stick
1 pint (2½ cups) brandy

Wash and dry the oranges and peel them carefully so that all the pith is removed. Cut the peel into fine stips and put in a wide-necked glass jar. Squeeze the oranges and pour the strained juice over the peel. Meanwhile, melt the sugar in the water to form a clear syrup, remove it from the heat and allow to cool. Add the cooled syrup to the jar with the cinnamon stick and pour over the brandy. Give the ingredients a thorough stir, and cover it tightly. Leave it for at least 3 weeks before trying it. Once the fruit brandy is started, keep it going by adding a variety of fruit peel. Serve it directly from the bottle or if you prefer to drink it without the peel, strain it before use.

Note: One friend of mine who has kept a jar going for well over a year adds a few washed raisins or sultanas instead of syrup to sweeten it.

RICE WINE

The Chinese and Japanese drink and cook with rice wine or sake. It is the traditional drink served at weddings and feasts and was thought to be discovered when a chef in the Imperial Palace some 3,500 years ago accidentally left some rice soaking in water in an earthenware jar which started to ferment.

Rice wine can be bought in the West, although it is often quite difficult to obtain, and its nearest equivalent is a medium-dry sherry. This recipe for a home-made version was kindly sent to me by Tessa and Douglas Plowden of Bron-Niwl, whose 'yellow wine' is renowned throughout Wales! It makes a potent wine which can be drunk by itself or used in a marinade (see recipes for Drunken Chicken, Marinated Steak, Sweet and Sour Fish, Red Steamed Pork) and the sediment can be used to make a wine sediment paste (see page 19), for marinating with chicken or fish.

2 pounds (4 cups) sugar (see note)
1 gallon (20 cups) water
1 pound (3 cups) raisins, washed
  and drained
1 pound (2⅔ cups) ground rice
juice of 1 lemon or 1 teaspoon citric
  acid
1 teaspoon dried yeast

Dissolve the sugar in the water and slowly heat the water until it is lukewarm. Add the raisins, rice, lemon juice (or citric acid) and yeast and stir all the ingredients together. Remove the pan from the heat, pour mixture into an earthenware crock and store in a warm place. Stir it daily for 7 days. Strain the liquid through a piece of fine muslin into a fermentation jar and keep it in a warm place until it has stopped fermenting. Syphon off the wine into a clean jar (retaining the sediment for a separate paste) and cork it securely. Store the wine in a cool place until the liquid is completely clear. Syphon it into small bottles and drink or use as required.

Note: For a really sweet rice wine, use 2½ pounds (5 cups) of sugar.

LEMON BRANDY

This makes an interesting liqueur which is drunk either by itself or with soda and ice as a refreshing aperitif. It can also be used to flavour various puddings, particularly sorbets or fruit mousses. The lemon rinds should also be kept once the drink has been strained to be used as a marinade with chicken or stewed with fresh fruit.

4 lemons   *1 pint (2½ cups) brandy or vodka*
                                              or white wine

Wash and dry the lemons. With a sharp knife peel them thinly so that there is no white pith, and cut the peel into fine strips. Put the peel in a wide-necked bottle and pour over the brandy. Cork the bottle securely and leave it to infuse for about 3 weeks. After that time strain the liqueur, return it to the bottle and use it as required. Retain the lemon peel and store it in a small, airtight container either covered in oil (for savoury dishes) or honey melted with a little water (for sweet dishes).

Oven temperature chart

	GAS MARK	°FAHRENHEIT	°CENTIGRADE
Very slow	¼	225	110
	½	250	130
Slow	1	275	140
	2	300	150
Warm	3	325	170
Moderate	4	350	180
Fairly hot	5	375	190
	6	400	200
Hot	7	425	220
Very hot	8	450	230
	9	475	240

Weights & measures

LIQUID MEASURES

¼ pint =   5 fl oz = 142 ml = ⅔ cup
½ pint = 10 fl oz = 284 ml = 1¼ cups
1 pint = 20 fl oz = 568 ml = 2½ cups

DRY MEASURES

Flour:	4 oz = 113 g = 1 cup = 16 tablespoons
Butter:	4 oz = 113 g = ½ cup = 8 tablespoons
Fresh vegetables, chopped	4 oz = 113 g = 1 cup
Cooked meat, chopped	8 oz = 226 g = 1 cup
Sugar, Salt	1 oz = 28 g = 2 tablespoons

INDEX